CW01524951

Beyond the Girl Dad

Guiding Your Daughter to Womanhood With Mindfulness, Effective Communication, and Peaceful Parenting

Jessica Sumner

Table of Contents

For MDW

Trigger warning: This book discusses themes of trauma and recovery that some readers may find distressing. Reader discretion is advised, especially for those with personal experiences related to trauma.

Introduction

Imagine a world where the phrase "just wait until your father gets home" brings smiles and excitement, not whispers of fear. Picture a father's role filled with as much nurturing and understanding as it is with protection and strength. This vision isn't just a dream—it's slowly becoming our new reality, thanks in part to the inspiring legacy of Kobe Bryant.

Kobe introduced us to the powerful concept of being a "girl dad," showcasing a relationship with his daughters that was not only loving but deeply empowering. This term, celebrated widely after his passing, symbolizes a father's pride and dedication to raising daughters who are confident, strong, and fearless.

So, why is this shift so important? Traditionally, fathers have been seen mainly as providers and protectors—roles that are undoubtedly important but can sometimes overshadow the equally critical needs for emotional openness and support. This old-school approach can unintentionally dampen a young girl's spirit and sense of autonomy, teaching her that her voice might be less valued than that of her male peers.

In this book, I invite you to join me on a personal journey inspired by my own experiences with an unenlightened father and a dominant mother. These reflections have fueled my passion to help fathers evolve into the supportive, understanding role models their daughters truly need. This book is crafted for dads who see themselves clinging to outdated roles and are eager for a change, aiming to enrich and balance their relationships with their daughters.

We'll start by exploring how the nervous systems of fathers and daughters interact, learning how stress and triggers influence these dynamics, and the foundational role this understanding plays in parenting. Then, we'll shift our focus to mindfulness, exploring it as a strategic response to stress. You'll learn about emotional regulation, lifestyle adjustments for stress management, and how to create a family stress reduction plan.

Next, we'll reflect on your personal parenting history and styles. Through various exercises, you'll gain insights into possibly reshaping your approach to parenting. Following that, our discussion will center on building communication bridges through mindfulness. Here, you'll see how effective communication strengthens your bond with your daughter and helps you navigate modern challenges like digital distractions.

Then, we move on to empowering your daughter's autonomy within a feminist framework. You'll discover how supporting her independence helps her thrive in a gender-equal world. Following this, we'll focus on supportive strategies for managing trauma, where you'll learn to understand, manage, and support your daughter through challenging times, ensuring she feels safe and nurtured.

Our journey concludes with comprehensive advice on supporting your daughter through critical life stages, with tips on fostering self-care, healthy relationships, and personal choices. By turning the pages of this book, you're setting the stage for profound changes. You'll deepen your relationship with your daughter, fostering an environment where she feels valued and empowered to express herself and chase her dreams.

I encourage you to reflect on your current parenting style as you engage with this book. Stay open to the transformative advice within these pages, and take an active role by participating in the exercises provided. Each chapter is designed to be interactive, encouraging you to apply these lessons in your daily life for real and immediate impact. Let's redefine what it means to be a "girl dad," transforming this role into a lifelong journey of learning, love, and mutual growth.

Chapter 1:

Nervous System Dynamics in Parent-Child Relationships

Ready to take the first step on a remarkable journey toward deepening your connection with your daughter? This chapter is designed to guide you through understanding the intricate dance of emotions and stress in your interactions. Your role is pivotal in shaping her emotional world, and it's here that we start by exploring the concepts of emotional intelligence and stress management.

Think of emotions as the heart of our relationships. They can light up our days or challenge us in complex ways. For fathers and daughters, navigating this emotional terrain requires a special kind of awareness and finesse. I'll guide you through how your own emotions and stress levels can impact your daughter and how you can use this insight to either strengthen your bond or, if not careful, strain it.

Getting a grip on emotional intelligence is essential. It does wonders for your ability to empathize and communicate effectively with your daughter. Plus, it prepares you to manage the stresses that naturally come with parenting. By tuning into your emotional habits and mastering them, you're setting up a safe space for her to grow, explore, and express herself freely—without fear of judgment or misunderstanding.

In this chapter, we'll go through some practical exercises to sharpen your emotional awareness. These are not just good for your relationship but are also crucial for your own emotional health. So, let's get started, shall we? Together, we're going to help you become the supportive, understanding, and compassionate father your daughter truly needs.

Understanding the Nervous System and Emotional Processing: The Key to Enhancing Father-Daughter Relationships

Emotions are these complex psychological states that really shape our daily lives—from what we decide to how we act and interact. They are multifaceted, encompassing a subjective experience, a physiological response, and a behavioral expression. This complexity is crucial in understanding father-daughter relationships, as it affects how you can effectively connect with and support your daughter throughout their growth into womanhood.

What Are Emotions?

Think of emotions as reactions we experience in response to various events or situations, triggered by our perception of those events. For instance, joy might erupt from receiving good news, while fear could be sparked by a threat. In this context, we're using the terms "emotions" and "feelings" interchangeably. These emotional reactions are not just fleeting feelings but are powerful drivers that influence our behavior and decision-making every day (Cherry, 2023).

The Role of the Nervous System in Emotional Processing

To fully appreciate how emotions function, it's essential to understand the nervous system's role. The human nervous system is divided into two main parts: the central nervous system (CNS), which includes the brain and spinal cord, and the peripheral nervous system (PNS), which comprises all other neural elements. Emotions are processed through a complex interaction between these two systems.

The CNS plays a pivotal role in interpreting emotional stimuli and coordinating responses. Within the CNS, the brain's limbic system—particularly the amygdala—is crucial for emotional processing. When you encounter an emotional stimulus, the amygdala evaluates its significance and triggers an appropriate emotional response. This process involves both "bottom-up" signals from the PNS providing sensory input to the brain and "top-down" signals from the CNS that can modify peripheral responses, enhancing our reaction to emotional stimuli (Pace-Schott et al., 2019).

What Happens in Our Bodies and Minds?

Emotions manifest through both physiological and psychological responses. Physiologically, emotions can trigger changes in heart rate, blood flow, and energy levels, all of which are mediated by the autonomic nervous system, a part of the PNS. This system regulates involuntary body functions, like heart rate and digestion, and is critical in the fight-or-flight response—a physiological reaction to perceived harmful events, attacks, or threats to survival.

Psychologically, emotions influence our thoughts and behaviors. For example, anxiety might lead to avoidance behaviors, while joy could encourage social interaction. These responses are crucial for survival, helping us navigate complex social environments and personal relationships.

Emotions as Communication Tools

One of the most significant roles of emotions is their function as communication tools. They signal to others our feelings and intentions and play a vital role in social interactions and personal relationships. In father-daughter relationships, being able to express and read emotional cues accurately can strengthen the bond.

Emotional expressions like a smile or a frown convey feelings and intentions that are universally recognized and provide a nonverbal means of communication that is vitally important in maintaining and strengthening relationships.

Good communication is crucial, especially when it comes to discussing emotional states. Openly sharing feelings helps fathers and daughters understand each other better. It fosters a sense of trust and safety, allowing for a deeper connection. For instance, when you acknowledge your daughter's feelings and respond empathetically, it shows you value her emotions. This recognition encourages her to be more open, leading to a stronger, more communicative relationship.

Planting the seed of good communication, especially when it comes to emotions, can transform the father-daughter dynamic. In the upcoming chapters, we'll explore the art of communication further to enhance our understanding and strengthen our connections.

The Interaction Between Basic and Advanced Brain Functions

Isn't it fascinating to see how our brains manage both survival instincts and complex thinking? The basic brain functions, particularly those centered around the limbic system and notably the amygdala, spring into action without hesitation when we face emotional triggers. These instant reactions are our body's rapid response system, essential for protecting us from immediate dangers.

Then we have the advanced brain functions located in the prefrontal cortex. This part of the brain steps in with more calculated and thoughtful responses, considering the long-term impacts and planning ahead. It's like having a wise strategist alongside a quick-reacting guard within the same control center.

According to Murray and Fellows (2021), the interplay between these brain regions helps us adapt to various situations, balancing immediate survival with longer-term goals. This dynamic is crucial not only for responding to life's challenges but also in social interactions and maintaining relationships, including with our children.

As dads, understanding this balance can help us recognize when to let our quick instincts take charge and when to slow down and think things through. This awareness can improve how we communicate with our kids, leading to deeper connections. It teaches us—and them—about the value of both genuine emotional reactions and thoughtful decision-making, nurturing a healthy blend that's essential for real-life situations.

The Power of Emotional Intelligence in Parenting

Now that we understand how emotions and the nervous system work together, let's explore how emotional intelligence (EI) can transform parenting. EI refers to the ability to recognize, understand, manage, and use emotions effectively in yourself and others. In the context of parenting, it becomes a cornerstone for nurturing a supportive and positive environment for your daughter's growth.

Recognizing and Understanding Emotions

The first step in bringing EI into your parenting is to get a handle on both your own emotions and your daughter's. This involves noticing how emotions show up in both physical and psychological ways and seeing how they affect thoughts and behaviors. For instance, you might need to spot when your own stress or frustration is coloring your reaction to something your daughter does or understand that her actions might be driven more by her feelings than her intentions.

Managing Emotions

Once you recognize and understand these emotions, the next step is to manage them effectively. This means regulating your own emotional responses and helping your daughter learn to manage hers. This skill is crucial because it teaches her how to handle emotions constructively rather than being overwhelmed by them. For instance, if a father remains calm and supportive when his daughter is upset, he not only avoids escalating the situation but also models how she can calm herself in stressful situations.

Using Emotions to Enhance Relationships

EI also involves using emotions to facilitate better interactions and strengthen relationships. It's about tapping into empathy to really connect with your daughter, to grasp what she's feeling and see things from her perspective, and then respond in a way that's right for the moment. When dads apply EI in their interactions, it builds a foundation of trust and understanding. This makes for a safe space where open conversations can happen, making everyone feel valued and connected and deepening the relationship.

Imagine your daughter is dealing with a tough situation at school. By applying EI, you can guide her to express what she's feeling, look at the situation from different angles, and work with her to figure out the best way to handle it. This doesn't just sort out the issue at hand; it also arms her with the skills to tackle future challenges on her own.

Long-Term Benefits

The benefits of applying EI in parenting extend far beyond immediate family interactions. For daughters, having an emotionally intelligent father can lead to better social skills, higher self-esteem, and improved mental health (Rasouli et al., 2018). These benefits can help her build more successful and satisfying relationships, both now and in her future professional and personal life.

Unraveling Stress and Its Unique Impact on the Father-Daughter Dynamic

Continuing from our exploration of EI and its significance in parenting, let's explore a specific emotional response that is both common and impactful: stress. Understanding stress—what it is, how it's different from other emotional responses, and how it affects both body and mind—can really change the way you handle your own stress and how you support your daughters through theirs.

What Exactly Is Stress?

Stress is essentially your body's way of responding to any kind of demand or threat. When you feel stressed, your body might react with physical, emotional, or psychological changes that make you feel threatened or upset. Stress can be triggered by a variety of events, from daily responsibilities like work and family to major life changes such as moving house or facing significant financial pressures.

Stress differs from other emotional responses because it can build up over time, leading to both short-lived (acute) and long-lasting (chronic) effects. Acute stress happens in quick bursts—think of dodging a car accident—and while intense, it usually fades quickly.

Chronic stress, however, sticks around and can build up when ongoing problems like job insecurity or chronic illness don't seem to have an end in sight.

Acute vs. Chronic Stress

Acute stress is your body's immediate response to a threat, kicking off the fight-or-flight reaction we've already talked about. It's designed to help us deal with immediate dangers and, while intense, usually doesn't last long.

Chronic stress, however, is more insidious and dangerous. It develops when there is no clear end to a stressor in sight and the body remains in a heightened state of stress for an extended period of time. This can wear down the body's resilience, potentially leading to serious health problems such as heart disease, high blood pressure, diabetes, and other illnesses, as well as mental health challenges like depression and anxiety (Franklin et al., 2021).

Physical and Psychological Responses to Stress

Physically, stress might show up as headaches, muscle tension, fatigue, and sleep disturbances. Psychologically, stress can manifest as irritability, anxiety, depression, and difficulty concentrating. For dads, these symptoms can change the way you parent, often leading to less patience and more reactive behavior, which might even pass the stress on to your daughters (Sharry, 2024).

For daughters, stress might manifest differently depending on their age and developmental stage. Younger children may exhibit stress through changes in their eating and sleeping habits or through more clingy, dependent behavior. Teenage daughters might display irritability, withdrawal from family activities, or a decline in academic performance. Recognizing these signs early on is crucial for fathers to effectively address and mitigate their effects.

The Big Picture: Stress and Parenting

The implications of stress on parenting are significant. It can make it harder for you to respond with empathy to your daughter's needs. When you're stressed, it might be tough to use those EI skills we talked about, like managing your emotions or using them positively in your interactions. This can create a cycle where stress leads to more stress, affecting everyone's mental health and overall well-being.

Understanding Common Triggers and Crafting Responses

Parenting is an immensely rewarding journey, yet it comes with its own set of unique stressors that can impact both the parent and child. For fathers, understanding these stressors, how they affect their daughters, and learning to manage them proactively is crucial for nurturing a healthy relationship.

Typical Stressors for Dads

- **Balancing work and family:** One of the biggest sources of stress for fathers is the need to balance the demands of a career with the responsibilities of family life. This challenge is exacerbated by traditional expectations that fathers should act as the primary providers for their families. The pressure to succeed professionally can often conflict with the desire to be present and actively engaged at home. Managing this balance requires time management and emotional energy, as fathers must shift gears between the competitive, often rigid world of work and the nurturing, flexible role required at home.

- **The role of the primary provider:** The traditional view of the father as the primary provider is still prevalent in many cultures and societies. This can pile on the pressure, making you feel like you're constantly falling short in securing your family's financial future—especially during economic downturns or times of financial uncertainty. This kind of stress can take a toll on your mental health and how emotionally available you are to your family.

- **Worries about children's futures:** Concerns about your daughters' futures—like their education, social life, emotional growth, and career opportunities—can also be a major source of stress. Wanting to give your kids the best possible chances can lead to a lot of second-guessing about whether you're making the right choices in guiding their paths.

- **Everyday logistical challenges:** Then there's the day-to-day logistics of parenting—managing schedules, keeping up with school events, and maintaining a stable home environment. For dads already stretched thin by work, these tasks, while mundane, demand constant attention and energy, adding to your overall stress load.

- **Maintaining household stability:** Ensuring that everything at home runs smoothly, from handling repairs and upkeep to managing finances and planning ahead, is crucial. The drive to maintain a stable, happy home is a persistent stressor, especially when unexpected challenges pop up, like health issues or household emergencies.

Diverse Family Structures and Their Unique Stressors

The family structure can significantly influence the stressors a father faces. For example, single fathers may experience unique challenges as they often have to take on dual roles. When you're a single dad, especially to a daughter, you might find yourself having to be both mother and father, fulfilling all parental responsibilities alone when she's in your care. This can intensify stress due to the pressure to perform well in both nurturing and providing roles without the support of a partner.

In heterosexual couple dynamics, stress might be distributed differently, often influenced by traditional roles or shared responsibilities. However, each parent might still face stress related to how to best support each other while managing their own contributions to parenting and household duties.

In same-sex couple dynamics, parents may face societal prejudices in addition to the usual challenges of parenting. These stressors can include external pressures from social, legal, and familial expectations, which can affect how they support each other while managing their contributions to parenting and household duties.

In blended families, where step-parents and step-siblings are involved, new layers of stress can emerge. Navigating relationships with stepchildren, aligning parenting styles with a step-partner, and maintaining peace and fairness in a newly mixed family requires a delicate balance that can be a significant source of stress.

Each of these structures brings unique challenges, and recognizing the specific pressures of your family setup can help in finding the most effective ways to manage stress and nurture a positive, healthy environment for your daughter.

How You React Matters: Addressing Negativity Bias

Fathers' reactions to their daughters' emotions can vary widely, but a common pattern includes a negativity bias. This negativity bias means you might dwell on the bad behaviors or moods and miss the good stuff. This usually comes from your own stress and worries, leading to less supportive or constructive reactions. For instance, if you're stressed, you might snap at your daughter over her homework frustrations instead of approaching the situation with patience and understanding, which just ramps up the stress for both of you.

How Stress Affects Your Kids

Children, especially those sensitive to emotional cues, can often detect stress in their parents, even if it's not talked about. This sensitivity can lead them to internalize the stress, affecting their own emotional and psychological state. For daughters, seeing their father stressed can lead to feelings of anxiety and helplessness, and in an attempt to cope, they might withdraw emotionally or exhibit behavioral changes such as increased irritability or aggression.

When children are exposed to stress, especially consistently, it doesn't just influence their mood—it can actually affect their brain development. During these formative years, their brains are like sponges, not only soaking up knowledge and behaviors but also reacting to emotional climates. Chronic stress can impact areas of the brain like the hippocampus, which is crucial for learning and memory, and the amygdala, which regulates emotions and stress responses (Cross et al., 2017). Changes here can lead to difficulties in school, such as trouble with concentration and memory or heightened emotional reactions that might seem disproportionate to the situation.

Moreover, the prefrontal cortex, which is responsible for decision-making and self-control, develops throughout childhood and well into young adulthood. High stress levels can hinder its development, making it harder for children to make thoughtful decisions or manage their impulses effectively. This is why sometimes, when a child is under a lot of stress, they might seem more prone to outbursts or unable to handle minor setbacks.

Cortisol, the body's stress hormone, plays a pivotal role in this process. While it's essential for managing acute stress, prolonged exposure to high levels of cortisol can be damaging. It can weaken the immune system, reduce overall brain function, and increase the risk of numerous health problems later in life.

This understanding of the neurobiological effects of stress underscores the importance of a mindful, nurturing approach to parenting. It's not just about avoiding negative outcomes; it's about actively contributing to your child's healthy emotional and psychological development, setting them up for a resilient and balanced life.

Stress Triggers in Daughters

Your daughter faces her own unique stressors that deeply influence how she expresses her emotions. These triggers often include:

1. **Societal influences:** Media portrayals of ideal lifestyles and appearances can place immense pressure on young girls, leading to stress and issues with self-esteem and body image.

2. **Peer pressure:** As daughters grow, especially during their teenage years, the influence of peers can become a major source of stress. The desire to fit in and be accepted can lead to emotional turmoil, especially if they feel they do not measure up to their peers in some way.

3. **Developmental stages:** Each stage of a daughter's development brings its own challenges. For instance, the onset of puberty can bring about a host of emotional, physical, and psychological changes that can be stressful for both the daughter and the father.

Understanding these stress triggers, recognizing how they show up in your daughter's life, and knowing how your reactions can either ramp up or reduce these stressors are vital. This understanding is your first step toward opening up empathetic and supportive conversations—key for both of your emotional well-being and for keeping your relationship strong.

Practical Exercises for Emotional Awareness: Recognizing Your Triggers

Ever wonder what really sets off your stress on a day-to-day basis? Let's dive into some simple yet powerful exercises to help you become more aware of your emotional triggers. These activities focus on self-assessment and journaling, offering you structured ways to get to know and manage your feelings better.

Daily Emotional Check-In

Why not start each day with a quick emotional pulse check? Find a quiet space, take a few deep breaths, and ask yourself:

- **How am I feeling today?** Reflect on your immediate emotional state. Are you feeling anxious, tired, excited, or perhaps a bit indifferent? Recognizing your current emotions is the first step toward understanding them.

- **What is my emotional state as I start the day?** Think about the mood that's coloring your feelings as you start your day. Are you dreading the pile of tasks waiting for you, or are you still annoyed about something that happened yesterday? Or maybe you're feeling upbeat and ready to jump into whatever the day throws at you. Knowing this can help you plan how to tackle the day's events.

These morning check-ins can clue you in on how to adjust your approach to whatever the day might bring. Feeling anxious? Maybe slot in something calming early in the day. Super charged up? That could be your cue to knock out some of those big tasks.

Stressor Identification Journal

Keep a handy notebook or a digital note app to jot down moments when you feel stressed. Whenever you catch yourself feeling irritable, fatigued, or anxious, make a note of:

- **The situation:** What exactly happened? Try to be specific. Instead of just "at work," maybe it was "during the budget meeting with the boss at 10 a.m."

- **Your emotions:** How did you feel during that moment? Frustrated, overwhelmed, or maybe a mix of feelings? Pinning down your emotions helps you understand what bothered you the most.

- **Your reaction:** How did you respond, both inside and out? Did you snap at someone, withdraw, or start feeling a headache brewing? Tracking your reactions helps you see if they're working for you or if there's room for improvement.

Trigger Mapping

Once you have a few entries in your stressor identification journal, use them to create a trigger map to identify patterns. On a large piece of paper, write down all identified triggers and categorize them into themes (work-related, family, financial, etc.). This visual representation helps in understanding which areas of your life contribute most to your stress and might need more focused attention or changes.

Steps to Create a Trigger Map

1. Gather your data: Start by reviewing your stressor identification journal. Pull out all the instances where you've noted feelings of stress and what caused them.

2. Categorize the triggers: Identify common themes or categories among these triggers. Typical categories might include:

- **Work-related:** Deadlines, workload, meetings, interactions with colleagues, career progression concerns.

- **Family:** Parenting challenges, partner relationships, health of family members.

- **Financial:** Budgeting issues, major purchases, savings, investment concerns.

- **Personal health:** Lack of sleep, poor diet, lack of exercise, medical concerns.

- **Social:** Interactions with friends, social obligations, feeling of belonging.

- **Other:** Any other categories specific to your lifestyle or experiences, such as educational pursuits or spiritual growth.

3. Create your map: Take a large piece of paper or a whiteboard and draw a circle in the middle labeled "Me." Around this central circle, draw several other circles, each labeled with one of the categories you identified.

4. Populate the map: Inside each category circle, write down specific triggers you've identified from your journal. For example, under Work-Related, you might write "urgent projects," "email overload," or "performance reviews."

5. Analyze connections: Draw lines to connect triggers that might be related. For example, "urgent projects" might connect to "lack of sleep" under Personal Health. This helps in identifying if one area of stress is exacerbating another.

6. Highlight key areas: Use different colors or markers to highlight the most frequent or intense triggers. This visual cue will help you quickly see which areas are contributing the most to your stress levels.

7. Reflect and plan: Once your map is complete, take a step back and reflect on what it shows. Which areas have the most triggers? Are there unexpected connections? Use this map to plan strategies to address these stress points.

Reflection Prompts for Deeper Insight

At the end of each week, set aside some time to reflect on your journal entries using specific prompts. Ask yourself:

- What did I learn about my stress triggers this week?
- Were there any surprises in how I reacted to certain situations?
- What might I do differently based on this week's experiences?

By getting to know your stress triggers and reactions, you're setting the stage for managing your stress more effectively, which can lead to better mental health and stronger relationships.

Wrapping Up

As we close this chapter, we've taken some important steps together toward understanding the complex emotions within your relationship with your daughter. We've delved into the roots of stress, how it's perceived by your children, and how recognizing these dynamics can profoundly enhance your bond.

Looking ahead, you're now better equipped to handle and manage these stressors more effectively. We'll continue to build on this foundation with practical strategies that address stress as it arises and help prevent it. These approaches are designed to foster resilience and a deeper connection between you and your daughter, creating a nurturing environment that supports both of your emotional well-being.

Let's keep strengthening those emotional skills essential for a thriving father-daughter relationship. As we move forward, you'll learn how to transform potential stressors into opportunities for growth and deeper connection, using each challenge as a stepping stone to enhance your understanding and interactions.

Chapter 2:

From Stress to Mindful Parenting in Father-Daughter Relationships

Ready to take control of your emotions? This is where we explore the transformative power of mindfulness. This isn't just a practice—it's a way of being. It's about staying present and fully engaged, even during stressful times. By developing mindfulness, you'll learn to observe your emotions without judgment, providing a calm anchor in both calm and stormy moments. This skill allows you to meet your daughter's emotional expressions with understanding and care, rather than reactive stress.

Emotional regulation goes hand in hand with mindfulness. It involves understanding your feelings, identifying what triggers them, and learning how to respond in ways that are constructive rather than destructive. This chapter will teach you how to stabilize your emotions and demonstrate how you can guide your daughter in managing her feelings.

We'll also explore lifestyle changes that support emotional regulation and stress management. These include habits around sleep, exercise, and nutrition that can profoundly influence your emotional health. Together, we'll uncover strategies for effectively modeling these essential skills to your daughter. By the end of this chapter, you'll be equipped with the tools needed to transform stressful situations into opportunities for growth and connection.

Mindfulness: A Neuroscientific Perspective

Mindfulness, often hailed as a panacea for a range of psychological ailments, is particularly transformative in the realm of parenting. Neuroscientific research has illuminated how mindfulness recalibrates our brain, emphasizing areas integral to emotional regulation and response control—like the prefrontal cortex and amygdala. Engaging in mindfulness practices can dampen the hyper-reactivity of the amygdala, known for its role in processing fear and emotional responses, and enhance the function of the prefrontal cortex, which governs our ability to assess and modulate those responses (Turpyn et al., 2019).

This neurobiological shift is not just about becoming less reactive; it's about becoming more present, patient, and responsive. For fathers, this means being able to meet a child's emotional states not with immediate reactions but with thoughtful responses that acknowledge and address those emotions without escalating stress or tension.

Emotional Intelligence and Regulation: Connecting the Dots

In the last chapter, we explored emotional intelligence (EI) as the skill set that enables individuals to recognize, understand, manage, and use emotions effectively. Here, we learn how EI underpins emotional regulation—a critical aspect of mindful parenting. Emotional regulation involves managing your emotions to maintain equilibrium and achieve your goals, which, in the context of parenting, includes fostering a supportive and nurturing environment.

Mindfulness bridges EI and emotional regulation by training the brain to pause before responding, allowing space for a more considered approach that can differentiate between instinctive reactions and thoughtful responses. This is especially crucial in interactions with children and teens of varying ages, who may require different levels of sensitivity and types of support. For example, the impulsive emotions of a toddler might require immediate but gentle redirection, whereas a teenager's complex emotional landscapes might call for more dialogue and understanding.

From Reaction to Mindful Response

Let's think back to those instinctive reactions we talked about earlier. In the hustle and bustle of daily life, especially when stress levels are up, it's all too easy for us to react quickly and automatically. These reactions are driven by basic brain functions, particularly from areas like the amygdala, which are primed to switch us into fight, flight, or freeze mode at the hint of a threat. Remember, this isn't just a basic response, but a vital one that has helped humans survive throughout history.

But here's the flip side: the mindful responses driven by the advanced brain functions in regions like the cortex. These functions allow us to pause, reflect, and consider the broader implications of our actions. They're not necessarily better than basic functions; rather, they provide a different kind of response that you'll need to achieve your long-term goals, including effective parenting.

For dads, understanding this difference is crucial. It's about managing your own stress and showing your daughters how to handle emotions in a healthy way. When you choose to respond thoughtfully instead of just reacting on impulse, you're teaching a valuable lesson. You're demonstrating that even in the heat of the moment, emotions can be managed and expressed constructively. This is essential for kids as they learn to navigate their own emotional worlds.

Neuroplasticity and Long-Term Changes

Practicing mindfulness regularly doesn't just help you handle stress at the moment; it changes your brain over time—a concept known as neuroplasticity (Sansone, 2024). These changes enhance your ability to pay attention, regulate your emotions, and reduce stress. For dads, this means you can stay present, calm, and connected with your daughter, even when challenges come up.

And there's more good news. These changes go beyond just managing stress—they reshape the brain to boost empathy, improve decision-making, and strengthen self-regulation. This kind of neurological development can transform your parenting approach, making it more attuned and responsive rather than reactive or dismissive. By fostering this kind of relationship, you're not just helping yourself; you're also supporting your daughter's emotional and psychological growth in profound ways.

Modeling and Teaching Emotional Regulation

When it comes to teaching your daughter how to manage her emotions, the saying "actions speak louder than words" takes on a whole new level of meaning. As fathers, demonstrating calm and composed behavior in the face of stress is not just about keeping our cool; it's about setting a living example for your daughter. This practice of co-regulation is vital, as it involves managing your own emotional responses to help your daughters learn to do the same.

For instance, imagine you're stuck in traffic and running late to a family event. A typical reaction might be frustration or even anger. However, by taking a deep breath, turning on some music, and using the time to chat about the day, you demonstrate how to handle stress positively. This doesn't just help you; it shows your daughter a practical way to deal with similar situations.

On the flip side, suppose you lose your temper. It happens to everyone. This is also a moment for co-regulation but in a different way. Later, you can talk to your daughter about the incident, explaining what triggered your reaction and how you could have handled it differently. Discussing both the misstep and the reflection allows her to see that emotional regulation isn't about being perfect; it's about making choices to manage feelings constructively, even after a slipup.

Through these everyday interactions, whether they're positive or a bit rocky, we're teaching our daughters important lessons about navigating their emotions, providing them with the tools they need to face their own challenges as they grow.

Practical Tips for Effective Modeling

Be the Calm in the Storm

One of the most powerful ways a father can teach his daughter about emotional regulation is by embodying calmness during stressful situations. This doesn't mean hiding emotions but rather showing how to manage them constructively.

- **Self-awareness:** Begin by recognizing your emotional triggers and the physical signs of stress in your body. This awareness will help you take proactive steps before emotions escalate.

- **Mindful pauses:** Incorporate pauses in your daily routine, especially during high-stress moments. A simple pause to take a deep breath or count to ten before reacting can model a thoughtful response over an impulsive reaction.

Consistency Is Key

Consistency in how emotions are handled at home creates a predictable environment that helps children feel secure. This security is foundational for them to explore their own emotions safely.

- **Routine practices:** Establish regular routines that incorporate emotional health practices, such as evening discussions about the highs and lows of the day or starting the day with a positive affirmation or a mindfulness moment.

- **Set clear expectations:** Clearly communicate the behaviors and responses that are expected in various situations. When deviations occur, discuss these instances openly to reinforce learning and understanding.

- **Maintain emotional boundaries:** Uphold boundaries around emotional expressions. For example, stating that it's okay to feel angry, but it's not okay to throw things in anger. This helps children differentiate between feeling emotions and expressing them in harmful ways.

Use Positive Reinforcement

Positive reinforcement is a splendid tool for teaching emotional regulation, especially when encouraging children to manage and express their feelings constructively. Essentially, it means you reward the behaviors you want to see more of. When your daughter handles a challenging situation well or healthily expresses her feelings, acknowledging this with praise, a hug, or even a small reward can make a big difference.

For example, say your daughter gets upset but takes a few moments to calm herself down before talking about what's bothering her. You could say, "I'm really proud of you for taking some deep breaths before we talked. That was a great way to handle your feelings." This kind of feedback encourages her to manage her emotions similarly in the future because she sees it makes you proud and earns her positive attention.

Using positive reinforcement doesn't just help in managing emotions; it also strengthens your bond with your daughter and builds her confidence. It makes her feel supported and valued, creating a nurturing environment where she can thrive emotionally.

Celebrate Small Wins

Building on this idea of using positive reinforcement, it's important to recognize and celebrate even the small achievements your daughter makes in managing her emotions. Children really thrive when they feel acknowledged and appreciated by their parents. This is especially true in the realm of emotional regulation, which can be tricky to master.

- **Immediate praise:** When you notice your daughter handling a disappointment well or expressing her feelings appropriately, praise her right then and there. A simple "I'm really proud of how you shared your feelings just now" can boost her confidence.

- **Share the achievement:** Make it a point to share these small wins with other family members during dinner or family gatherings to show her that her efforts are valued.

- **Reward with quality time:** Sometimes, the best reward is your time. Consider setting aside special time to do something she loves as a way to celebrate her progress. Whether it's a game night, a bike ride, or reading together, linking these activities to her emotional achievements reinforces the value of her efforts.

Encouragement Jars

Visual tools like encouragement jars can be incredibly effective for children, making the concept of emotional regulation tangible and rewarding.

- **Creating the jar:** Let her decorate a small jar or box where these notes will be kept. This makes the jar personally significant to her and more engaging.

- **Writing notes together:** Occasionally, sit down with her to write these notes together. Discuss instances when each of you felt proud of handling a difficult situation well. This not only helps her recognize her own strengths but also sees you practicing what you preach.

- **Reviewing the jar:** Make a routine, maybe once a month, where you both sit and read through the notes in the jar. It's a heartwarming way to reflect on the positive steps she's taken and reinforce the good habits she's developing.

Lifestyle Changes for Enhanced Stress Management

Managing stress and regulating emotions isn't just about mindfulness and positive reinforcement; it involves a holistic approach that incorporates essential lifestyle changes. You can significantly enhance your ability to handle stress and manage emotions effectively by focusing on sleep, nutrition, and physical exercise.

Sleep: The Foundation of Emotional Well-Being

Sleep serves as a cornerstone for our emotional well-being. It's during those quiet hours that our brain busily processes the emotional content of the day, resetting and preparing us for the challenges ahead. Without adequate sleep, our ability to handle stress and emotionally charged situations diminishes significantly.

Practical Steps to Enhance Sleep for Emotional Well-Being

Now that we understand the why, let's talk about the how—how can we improve our sleep to support our emotional health? Here are some practical, sustainable steps:

- **Establish a sleep-conducive environment:** Your bedroom should be a sleep sanctuary. Keep it cool, dark, and quiet. Consider using blackout curtains, eye masks, or white noise machines to create an ideal sleeping environment.

- **Develop a relaxing bedtime routine:** Just as children benefit from bedtime routines, so do adults. Engage in relaxing activities before bed, like reading, taking a warm bath, or practicing relaxation exercises. Avoid screens and other stimulating activities that can make it harder to fall asleep.

- **Stick to a sleep schedule:** Consistency is key in building and maintaining good sleep habits. Adjust your sleep schedule to consistently go to bed and rise at the same times daily, including weekends. This practice stabilizes your body's internal clock, enhancing your ability to fall asleep and wake up more effortlessly.

- **Mind what you eat and drink:** Avoid heavy meals, caffeine, and alcohol before bedtime. These can disrupt sleep by causing discomfort, increasing wakefulness, or altering the natural stages of sleep.

- **Limit daytime naps:** While naps can be a great way to catch up on missed sleep, long or irregular napping during the day can negatively affect your nighttime sleep pattern.

Incorporating these practices into your daily routine can significantly impact your emotional and psychological well-being. Remember, sleep isn't just a period of inactivity; it's an active, vital process for emotional and physical health. By prioritizing good sleep hygiene, you're not just investing in better nights but also happier, more resilient days.

Nutrition: Fueling Emotional Stability

Every meal you consume can be a stepping stone toward better emotional regulation. Foods rich in nutrients contribute to the overall health of your brain, affecting how you handle stress and regulate emotions. It's not just about the calories or the pleasure of eating; it's about fueling the brain in ways that support balanced mood and emotional resilience.

- **Boosting brain function:** Foods high in omega-3 fatty acids, like salmon and flaxseeds, are known for their role in brain health. These fats are essential for the maintenance of brain cells and can help enhance the function of neurotransmitters, which in turn supports emotional regulation and reduces mood swings (Santos et al., 2022).

- **Stabilizing blood sugar:** You know that sluggish feeling after a big, sugary meal? That's a blood sugar crash, and it can wreak havoc on your mood. Foods with a low glycemic index, such as whole grains and legumes, release glucose slowly into the bloodstream, which helps maintain stable energy levels and mood throughout the day.

- **Enhancing gut health:** The gut is often called the "second brain" for a reason. A healthy gut contributes to a strong immune system and produces many of the same neurotransmitters found in the brain, including serotonin, which significantly impacts our mood. Eating a diet rich in fiber, fermented foods, and leafy greens can help foster a healthy gut microbiome, which in turn supports emotional well-being.

Practical Tips for Eating Your Way to Emotional Stability

So, how can you leverage nutrition to enhance both your emotional regulation and your children's? Here are some actionable tips:

- **Incorporate a variety of nutrients:** Strive for a diverse palette in your meals—incorporate fruits, vegetables, whole grains, and lean proteins to create a balanced and mood-boosting diet.

- **Mindful eating:** Notice how various foods impact your mood and energy. Keeping a food diary can help you identify patterns and make adjustments. It's not just what you eat, but also how you eat—eating slowly and mindfully can enhance digestion and the absorption of nutrients.

- **Hydration:** Don't forget about water! Staying hydrated helps everything, from your brain to your metabolism, function better. Sometimes, dehydration can even masquerade as feelings of anxiety or irritability.

- **Limit processed foods:** While they're convenient, processed foods often lack essential nutrients and are high in sugars and fats that can lead to energy spikes and crashes, impacting your mood and emotional responses.

- **Plan for regular meals and snacks:** Skipping meals can lead to blood sugar dips and mood swings. Regular meals and healthy snacks can keep your blood sugar stable and your mood even.

For parents, understanding the impact of nutrition on emotion regulation extends to feeding practices with their children. Responsive feeding—recognizing and responding appropriately to a child's hunger and fullness cues—encourages healthier eating patterns and emotional relationships with food.

However, the opposite practices, like pressuring children to eat or imposing strict food restrictions, can disrupt these natural cues. According to Santos et al. (2022), such nonresponsive feeding practices are linked not only to poor emotion regulation but also to unhealthy eating patterns that may persist over time.

The study highlights how children with better emotion regulation skills tend to have healthier eating behaviors. This is likely because these children are better at managing their feelings without resorting to food as a comfort mechanism, a habit known as emotional eating. Conversely, children who struggle with emotion regulation may turn to unhealthy foods—high in sugars and fats—to cope with their emotions. This can lead to a cycle where emotional distress is temporarily relieved by such foods, reinforcing the habit.

For example, if a child feels anxious or upset and is given sweets to calm down, they might start associating sweet treats with comfort from their distress. Over time, this can lead to preferences for unhealthy foods, which affects their physical health and their ability to regulate emotions effectively. In contrast, children who are encouraged to express their emotions and are supported through responsive feeding practices are more likely to develop both healthier eating habits and better emotional coping strategies.

Fostering an environment where children can learn to listen to their bodies and enjoy a variety of foods contributes to their emotional and physical health. Encouraging children to participate in choosing and preparing meals can also enhance their interest in healthy eating and develop their ability to regulate their emotions related to food.

Physical Exercise: A Natural Stress-Reducer

Regular physical activity tones your muscles, boosts your stamina, and does wonders for your emotional health. Have you ever felt a surge of good vibes after a brisk walk or a dance class? That's not just a coincidence; it's your body's natural response to exercise, helping you regulate emotions more effectively. So, why does this happen?

- **Boosts endorphins:** Exercise increases the production of endorphins, those feel-good neurotransmitters in the brain. Think of them as your body's natural painkillers. They play a key role in reducing stress and anxiety, helping you feel more relaxed and happy.

- **Enhances aerobic fitness:** Physical activities like jogging or cycling improve your aerobic fitness, which is linked to better emotional regulation. When your aerobic capacity increases, your body becomes better at managing the physiological aspects of stress and anxiety (Zhang et al., 2019).

- **Increases mindfulness:** Exercises strengthen the body and focus the mind. Most activities enhance your awareness and presence in the moment, which can significantly lower stress levels and improve your mood.

Examples to Get You Moving

- **Morning runs:** Start your day with a morning jog at a comfortable pace. Notice how the air feels, listen to the sounds around you, and observe the environment. This not only boosts your fitness but also clears your mind and prepares you for the day ahead.

- **Yoga breaks:** Incorporate short yoga sessions into your daily routine. These can be as simple as doing a few stretches and poses during a break at work or a quick session at home before dinner.

- **Dance it out:** Put on your favorite music and dance freely for a few minutes. Dancing can be an excellent way to express emotions and reduce stress, plus it's a fun way to get your body moving!

By integrating regular physical activity into your life, you're not just improving your physical health but also enhancing your ability to manage emotions effectively. Remember, the goal is to find activities that you enjoy, so you'll stick with them long-term. Embrace the journey of using exercise as a tool to boost both your mood and your overall well-being!

Sustainable Exercise Practices:

- **Start small:** If you're new to exercise, begin with small, manageable goals. A 10-minute walk around your neighborhood or a brief yoga session at home can be a great start. Why not invite your daughter to join you? It's a fun way to spend time together and introduce her to the benefits of staying active.

- **Incorporate variety:** Mix up your routine with different types of exercises—cardio, strength training, flexibility, and balance exercises—to keep things fresh and engaging for both you and your daughter. Trying new activities together can be a bonding experience that keeps both of you motivated.

- **Family activities:** Make physical activity a family affair. Plan regular hikes, bike rides, or games that get everyone moving. This sets a good example for your daughter and strengthens your emotional bond as you create lasting memories together.

- **Make it social:** Adding a social element to your exercise routine can boost your motivation and enjoyment. Consider joining group classes or sports teams together. Exercising with others, especially with your daughter or family friends, can provide a supportive community and make each workout feel like a fun event.

- **Consistency is key:** Sticking to a regular exercise schedule is crucial for emotional regulation. Establish a routine that fits easily into your family's life. Even committing to it three times a week can make a significant difference in how you and your daughter handle stress and emotional challenges.

- **Be mindful:** During exercise, encourage your daughter and yourself to focus on how your bodies feel with each movement. This practice of mindfulness during exercise deepens the physical benefits and enhances the emotional rewards, helping both of you to stay present and away from negative thoughts.

By adopting these practices, you're not just improving your own emotional and physical health; you're also guiding your daughter on the path to a healthier, happier life.

Integrating These Practices

Here's the secret: Incorporating better sleep, nutrition, and exercise supports each other. Better sleep improves your energy levels and mood, which makes you more likely to exercise. In turn, exercise can help you sleep better and eat more mindfully. It's a beneficial cycle that enhances your overall quality of life.

Ultimately, these lifestyle modifications create a stable foundation for you and your daughter to manage stress and to thrive emotionally, mentally, and physically. By demonstrating these habits and actively engaging in them together, you're setting an example for your daughter, showing her practical ways to nurture her own emotional and physical health as she grows.

Practical Exercises and Reflection: Crafting a Family Stress Reduction Plan

Introducing a family stress reduction plan isn't just about finding ways to unwind—it's about building a resilient, supportive family culture that can weather any storm together. Here are practical exercises and reflections designed to engage the entire family in identifying and managing stress collectively.

Family Stress Audit

Start by gathering everyone in the family for an open discussion about stress. Create a safe space where each person can talk about what has been stressing them out recently, without judgment or interruption. Use a whiteboard or large piece of paper to list these stressors. Seeing everything in one place helps to identify common sources of stress and acknowledge individual struggles.

- **Reflection:** After listing the stressors, ask each family member to reflect on how these stressors make them feel and what might help. This can include emotional feelings or physical sensations, helping to create a more profound understanding within the family about how stress affects each member differently.

Developing a Family Stress Management Toolbox

As a family, discuss and compile a list of activities and strategies that help alleviate stress. This toolbox might include activities like walking, biking, reading, yoga, or even watching movies together. Make sure to include activities that are both individual and group-based, allowing for personal time as well as family bonding.

- **Reflection:** Encourage each family member to choose an activity from the toolbox each week. Reflect at the end of the week on how engaging in these activities affected their stress levels. This reflection can be shared during a family meal or set meeting time, reinforcing the practice of open communication and mutual support.

Daily Gratitude Practice

Incorporate a daily gratitude session into your family routine, perhaps during dinner or right before bed. Each person shares something they were grateful for that day. This practice shifts focus from stress to appreciation, which can significantly improve mood and outlook.

- **Reflection:** Once a month, reflect on the gratitude shared and discuss any patterns or surprises in what family members are thankful for. This can open discussions about what brings joy to each person and how the family can support and create more of those joyful experiences together.

Stress Signal System

Create a family "stress signal" system where each member can indicate they are feeling overwhelmed without needing to articulate it fully at the moment. This could be a simple hand signal, a special word, or even a household item placed in a common area. This system helps in recognizing when someone needs space or extra support.

- **Reflection:** Regularly check in about how the stress signal system is working. Is it helpful? Do people feel supported when they use it? Make adjustments as needed based on the feedback to ensure it remains a useful tool for managing stress.

Establish Quiet Zones

Designate certain areas in the home as "quiet zones" where family members can go to escape the hustle and bustle of family life. These zones should be free from electronics, loud noises, and interruptions.

- **Reflection:** Regularly discuss how these quiet zones are being used and whether they are effective in providing a respite from stress. Consider rotating or redesigning these areas to keep them effective and inviting.

Role Reversal Scenarios: Understanding Stress Through Your Daughter's Eyes

Occasionally, engage in role reversal exercises where you imagine being in your daughter's place during stressful interactions. Write about:

1. How you might feel as she observes your stress.

    - As you step into your daughter's role, consider how it might feel to witness your stress. Children often perceive their parents' stress without fully understanding the causes, which can be confusing and alarming. As "her," you might feel helpless or worried, wondering why you are upset and whether you did something wrong. You might also feel a longing to help or make things better, coupled with uncertainty about what to do.

    - **Reflection:** After acting out her role, reflect on these feelings. How does it feel to see yourself stressed through her eyes? What emotions did this perspective stir in you? This reflection can help you grasp the emotional impact of your visible stress on your daughter.

2. How your reactions might affect her.

    - From her perspective, your reactions during stress—whether they involve raised voices, silent treatments, or anxious behaviors—might be interpreted in ways you didn't intend. For instance, if you tend to withdraw when stressed, she might feel she is being pushed away or that she is the cause of your distress. Conversely, if your stress manifests in irritability or anger, she might feel scared, blamed, or as though she needs to walk on eggshells around you.

- **Reflection:** Consider how these reactions might affect her sense of security and her behavior toward you and others. Does it make her more anxious? More prone to hide her feelings or lie to avoid triggering a stressful response? Reflecting on these questions can open your eyes to the critical influence your handling of stress has on her developing approach to her own emotions and challenges.

Use this newfound empathy to motivate changes in how you manage and express stress. Discuss with your daughter what you've learned from being "her" and ask for her feedback on what she needs from you when you're stressed. This conversation can lead to developing new strategies together, such as identifying signs that stress is escalating and agreeing on how to approach each other during these moments.

Wrapping Up

In this chapter, we've explored how mindfulness transforms parenting by enhancing emotional regulation and presence. Through mindfulness, you learn to manage stress effectively and respond to your daughter's needs thoughtfully, fostering a nurturing environment for her emotional growth. We've also touched on how sleep, nutrition, and exercise play crucial roles in supporting emotional health, offering practical tips to integrate these into your family life.

In the upcoming chapter, we'll delve deeper into understanding your own parenting roots, exploring how your experiences and influences shape your parenting style. This reflection is vital as it helps you recognize patterns, both beneficial and challenging, that you may unconsciously replicate in your interactions with your daughter. Your journey toward more mindful and effective parenting begins now—let's make it count!

Chapter 3:

Reflecting on Your Parenting Roots

Reflecting on your personal parenting history is like opening a book filled with stories that have shaped you. In this chapter, we go deep into these narratives to understand the behaviors and expectations you've inherited. This understanding isn't just about knowing where you come from; it's about choosing where you want to go, especially in your role as a father.

Think of this as an archaeological dig, where each layer reveals something new about why you parent the way you do. It's about recognizing patterns, both helpful and unhelpful, that have been passed down through generations. You gain the power to enhance what works and transform what doesn't by understanding these patterns and actively shaping a more effective and nurturing parenting style.

This process is about more than just breaking cycles or making changes—it's about creating a legacy of conscious, thoughtful parenting. It empowers you to be the father you truly want to be. Let's embark on this journey together, uncovering the past to build a better foundation for your relationship with your daughter and setting a new standard for the generations that will follow.

Exploring Parenting Styles: A Guide to Understanding and Adapting Your Approach

Before diving into your own parenting stories, let's lay the groundwork with a comprehensive look at the four primary parenting styles—authoritative, authoritarian, permissive, and uninvolved—and the impacts these styles have on children based on the insights by Pardee (2024). This exploration is crucial because the way you parent shapes your day-to-day interactions with your children and deeply influences their emotional and psychological development.

Authoritarian Parenting: Strict Rules, High Expectations

Authoritarian parenting is marked by a focus on obedience, discipline, and control. Parents who adopt this style often employ a "my way or the highway" approach, emphasizing strict rules and expecting compliance without question. These parents are less likely to consider their children's feelings or opinions, often responding with "because I said so" to any challenge to their rules.

- **Effects on children:** Children raised by authoritarian parents may obey while under close supervision but could rebel against authority when away from parental control. They often struggle with social skills, may have lower self-esteem, and exhibit issues such as hostility and aggression.

Permissive Parenting: Leniency and Friendliness

Permissive parents are characterized by leniency and a friendly, open approach. They set rules but rarely enforce them, acting more like friends than authority figures. This style involves minimal expectations and discipline, often leading to situations where children do as they please.

- **Effects on children:** Children of permissive parents may face difficulties with self-regulation and respect for authority. They often struggle with academic and social challenges due to a lack of boundaries and may develop issues like impulsiveness and poor emotional regulation.

Authoritative Parenting: Balance and Reason

Considered the "gold standard" of parenting, authoritative parenting combines high expectations with responsiveness to children's emotional needs. These parents set clear rules and guidelines but are also nurturing and supportive. They encourage independence while maintaining limits and structure, often using positive discipline strategies to guide behavior (Dewar, 2024).

- **Effects on children:** Kids raised by authoritative parents tend to be happy, successful, and well-adjusted. They usually have excellent social skills, self-esteem, and self-regulation abilities. They're also more likely to perform well academically and maintain healthy relationships.

Uninvolved Parenting: Neglect and Lack of Guidance

Uninvolved parenting, sometimes referred to as neglectful parenting, involves minimal involvement, nurturance, or guidance. Parents who use this approach tend to neglect their children's needs and often fail to establish clear boundaries or expectations. This approach can stem from a lack of knowledge about child development or from overwhelming personal issues that limit the parent's capacity to engage.

- **Effects on children:** Children of uninvolved parents frequently experience performance and emotional issues, such as poor academic performance, low self-esteem, and behavioral problems. They often exhibit difficulties in forming healthy relationships and may engage in delinquent behavior or substance abuse.

Sub-Types of Parenting Styles: Variations on a Theme

Beyond these core styles, parenting can also include subtypes such as helicopter, free-range, and tiger parenting, each with its own unique approach and implications:

- **Helicopter parenting:** Involves closely monitoring and often overprotecting children, potentially stifling their ability to engage in problem-solving and development of autonomy.

- **Free-range parenting:** Encourages children to function independently and with minimal parental supervision, promoting self-sufficiency and resilience.

- **Tiger parenting:** Emphasizes strict rules and high expectations, often leading to high academic achievement at the potential cost of psychological stress and reduced social competence.

Reflecting on Your Roots: Shaping Parenting Styles Through Self-Awareness

Understanding how your own upbringing influences your parenting style is essential as a father. Your parents' attitudes and behaviors have undoubtedly shaped your perceptions and actions, both positively and negatively. By diving deep into these influences, you can start to make more conscious choices about how you parent, ensuring that your methods align with the values you wish to instill in your daughter.

Understanding Inherited Traits and Behaviors

You bring a unique mix of traits and behaviors from your own upbringing into your role as a father. Some of these qualities might naturally enhance your parenting style, while others could pose challenges as you guide and teach your daughters. Recognizing these traits is the first step toward understanding how they manifest in your current parenting style.

- **Positive Influences:** Reflect on the aspects of your upbringing that you appreciate. Perhaps your father was incredibly supportive of your academic efforts, or your mother taught you the value of patience. These experiences will likely help you foster a nurturing and encouraging environment for your daughter.

- **Negative Influences:** It's also important to acknowledge and confront less beneficial behaviors that we've inherited. Maybe you grew up in a household where shouting was the norm during disagreements, or perhaps there was a lack of open communication. Recognizing these patterns allows us to actively choose not to perpetuate them.

Beyond your direct familial lineage, various factors can subtly—or not so subtly—influence your parenting styles. It's essential to acknowledge the broader societal, cultural, and environmental influences that also play a role in shaping how you parent. Here's a deeper dive into these additional influences and how they can affect your approach to fatherhood.

- **Cultural influences:** Culture profoundly shapes our beliefs about parenting, discipline, education, and what we consider "normal" or acceptable behavior for children and their parents. These cultural norms can affect how you express affection, manage discipline, and set expectations for your children. For instance, some cultures emphasize collective family achievements and interdependence, while others may prioritize individualism and personal success.

- **Societal expectations:** Society often has clear expectations about the roles fathers should play in their children's lives. These expectations can influence how you engage with your daughters, from the activities you choose to the emotional support you offer. Societal norms about masculinity, for example, can affect whether fathers feel comfortable openly expressing emotions or engaging in nurturing behaviors.

- **Economic factors:** The economic situation can also significantly impact your parenting style. Financial security allows fathers to provide more opportunities for their children and can reduce stress in family life. Conversely, economic stress can lead to increased parental stress and anxiety, which might manifest as impatience or withdrawal in parenting interactions.

- **Educational backgrounds:** Level of education can influence parenting style in various ways. It can determine your expectations for your children's academic achievements, your approaches to learning, and the resources you use to support your children's education. Parents with higher educational attainments are often more likely to engage in "concerted cultivation," actively fostering and nurturing their children's talents and academic opportunities (Carolan & Wasserman, 2015).

- **Personal experiences:** Life experiences, such as travels, relationships, and careers, enrich your perspectives and indirectly influence your parenting. For example, fathers who have had positive sports experiences might be more likely to encourage physical activities for their children. Similarly, those who have benefited from a strong mentor might value fostering similar relationships for their children.

- **Community environment:** The community in which you live plays a crucial role in shaping your parenting. Communities can offer support networks, resources, and a sense of belonging, which can enhance your parenting practices. However, communities can also present challenges such as negative peer influences or limited access to resources, which might necessitate different kinds of parenting strategies to navigate.

- **Media influence:** In today's digital age, media is a pervasive force that can influence parenting styles through the portrayal of family dynamics, parenting norms, and children's behavior in television shows, movies, and social media. These portrayals can set unrealistic expectations or provide diverse perspectives on parenting challenges and solutions.

Understanding these layers of influence can provide a more comprehensive view of the factors that shape your parenting approaches. Recognizing them allows you to adapt more consciously and perhaps choose differently from what you have unconsciously absorbed from your environment.

Interactive Exercise: Assessing Your Parenting Style

Understanding your own parenting style is transformative. This interactive exercise is designed to help you delve deeper into your current approach, recognize patterns, and perhaps even pave the way for adjustments that align better with your aspirations as a father.

Step 0: Identifying Your Core Values

Before we explore your parenting style, it's essential to start with the foundation—your core values. Understanding what you value most will guide your decisions and interactions with your daughter. This step is about connecting deeply with what truly matters to you, ensuring that your parenting aligns with your deepest convictions.

Here's how to get started:

1. **List creation:** Take a moment to write down all the values you consider important. These might include honesty, responsibility, kindness, resilience, or any other values that resonate with you.

2. **Prioritization:** Look at your list and choose the top 5 values that are most critical to you. These are values you cannot compromise on, ones that

you wish to instill in your daughter as she grows.

3. **Justification:** For each of the top 5 values, write a few sentences about why these are particularly important to you. This is not just about acknowledging these values but also understanding and articulating their significance in your life.

Step 1: Reflection Questions

Begin by answering these reflective questions honestly. You might find it helpful to write down your answers in a journal or a digital document.

1. **Describe a recent parenting challenge:** How did you handle it? What was your immediate reaction, and what was the outcome?

2. **Communication check:** Think about a typical day. How much time do you spend talking with your daughter? What are these conversations like?

3. **Discipline dynamics:** When it comes to discipline, what strategies do you find yourself using most often? Are they effective?

4. **Support and encouragement:** How do you support your daughter's interests and efforts? Give examples of how you have recently encouraged her.

5. **Rules and responsibilities:** What are the key rules in your household? How did you decide on these, and how are they enforced?

Step 2: Identify Your Style

Using your responses from the reflection questions, read through the descriptions of the four primary parenting styles below and see which one resonates most with your current practices:

- **Authoritarian:** You believe in strict rules and expect obedience without question. "Because I said so" is a common phrase in your household.
- **Permissive:** You are lenient, with few expectations or demands. You might often feel more like a friend than a parent.
- **Authoritative:** You enforce rules and give consequences, but you consider your daughter's feelings and explain the reasons behind your rules.
- **Uninvolved:** You are hands-off, with few interactions or engagements in your daughter's day-to-day life.

Step 3: Analyze the Fit

Reflect on the parenting style you identify with the most:

- Does it align with the values you wish to instill in your daughter?
- What aspects of this style do you appreciate, and which parts do you wish to change?

Shaping Your Aspirational Parenting Style

After reflecting on your current parenting style and the traits you've inherited, it's time to consider what your ideal, aspirational parenting style looks like. This is about envisioning a style that not only feels authentic to you but also meets the unique needs and personality of your daughter. This step is crucial—it's about setting a direction for personal growth that aligns with the kind of father you aspire to be.

Step 1: Envision Your Ideal Style

Start by imagining your ideal interactions with your daughter. Consider these questions to guide your thoughts:

- What kind of relationship do you want to have with your daughter?
- How do you want her to remember her childhood and your role in it?

- What values do you want to instill in her through your parenting?

Visualize scenarios where you are embodying this ideal style:

- How would you handle a disagreement?

- What does support look like in this ideal setting?

- How do you react to her achievements and mistakes?

Step 2: Consider Her Needs

Reflecting on your daughter's personality, age, and individual needs is essential in shaping your aspirational style. Each child is unique, and understanding her specific emotional, social, and developmental needs will help you tailor your parenting approach effectively.

- How does she respond to different types of discipline?

- What communication style is she most receptive to?

- What does she need most from you to feel secure and supported?

Step 3: Compare and Contrast

Now that you have a clear picture of your ideal parenting style and a deep understanding of your daughter's needs, compare this with your current parenting approach. Identify the gaps between your current style and your aspirational style.

- Are there specific behaviors or reactions that need modification?

- What inherited traits are helping or hindering your progress toward this ideal?

Step 4: Embrace Flexibility

While having a clear aspirational style is beneficial, it's equally important to remain flexible. Your daughter will grow and change, and so will her needs and your relationship. Being adaptable, learning from experiences, and being willing to adjust your methods are key aspects of a successful parenting strategy.

Start by making a habit of regularly checking in on your parenting approach. Ask yourself what's working, what isn't, and how your daughter's needs might have changed. This ongoing assessment will guide you in making necessary adjustments.

It is also important to plan for flexibility in your parenting strategy. While having some nonnegotiable rules is important, also recognize which areas allow for flexibility to accommodate special circumstances or changes in your daughter's life. Then answer:

- How will you stay responsive to changes in her needs as she grows?
- What strategies can you implement to remain adaptable in your parenting approach?

Step 5: Role Modeling

Consider how every action and decision you make can serve as a model for your daughter. Your approach to challenges, your interactions with others, and your self-care practices all teach her how to handle life's complexities.

- What behaviors do you want to model to encourage her to emulate them?
- How can you demonstrate the qualities you hope to instill in her?

Step 6: Family Feedback

Engage your daughter in a discussion about your parenting style. You can ask her:

- How do you feel about the rules at home?
- What can I do to make you feel more supported and understood?

- Is there anything about my parenting that you would like me to do differently?

Step 7: Creating a Plan and Setting Goals

With a clear vision of your aspirational parenting style and a deep understanding of your daughter's needs, it's time to lay out a strategic plan that bridges the gap between your current practices and where you aspire to be. This plan includes specific, actionable steps that will guide your daily interactions and long-term relationship with your daughter. Here's how to structure this crucial step:

- Identify books, courses, or articles that can enhance your understanding of her developmental stages. Staying informed about these will help you tailor your parenting approach more effectively.

- Determine which respectful and constructive discipline methods you can adopt. These should align with both your goals and her personality, ensuring they are effective without being oppressive.

- Set behavioral goals. For example, if you recognize a tendency toward authoritarianism, set a goal to engage in more democratic decision-making with your daughter.

- If you find that your current style doesn't adequately support her development, set goals to incorporate activities that boost her confidence and independence.

Remember to keep a reflective journal, have regular check-ins with yourself, and, when appropriate, with your daughter about how the changes are affecting your relationship. This ongoing process of reflection and adjustment ensures that you remain aligned with your aspirational style while meeting the evolving needs of your daughter.

Envisioning Your Ideal Parenting Journey: Visualization Exercises for Fathers

Visualization is a powerful tool, not just for athletes or entrepreneurs but for parents, too. By imagining the type of parent you want to be, you can start shaping your behavior to align with this vision. These exercises are designed to help you visualize both the daily interactions and the long-term relationship you aspire to have with your daughter. Focusing on emotional responses and conflict resolution strategies, these activities will guide you toward becoming the parent you truly want to be.

Daily Interactions Visualization

Exercise 1: The Morning Routine

1. **Set the scene:** Imagine it's a weekday morning. Visualize yourself and your daughter during the morning routine. See the environment around you—is it chaotic, calm, or joyful?

2. **Focus on interaction:** Picture a specific interaction, perhaps during breakfast or as you're saying goodbye before she heads to school. Imagine her expressing a concern about the day ahead.

3. **Respond mindfully:** Visualize how you want to respond. See yourself listening attentively, acknowledging her feelings, and offering supportive feedback. Imagine your tone of voice, your body language, and the words you choose.

4. **Visualize the outcome:** See her reaction to your response—perhaps a smile, a nod, or a relieved expression. Feel the connection and trust being built through this simple, supportive exchange.

Exercise 2: Homework Help

1. **Setting:** Visualize a common scenario, such as helping with homework. Picture the setting—

where are you sitting, what does the room look like, and what time of day is it?

2. **Challenge:** Imagine she encounters a problem she can't solve and starts to get frustrated. See her body language and hear her tone of voice expressing frustration.

3. **Envision your approach:** Picture yourself maintaining composure, offering encouragement, or suggesting a short break. Visualize yourself guiding her through the problem with patience and encouragement.

4. **Positive feedback:** As the session ends, see her feeling accomplished and thankful for your help. Notice the sense of satisfaction and connection you feel, reinforcing your role as her supportive guide.

Long-Term Relationship Visualization

Exercise 1: The Teenage Years

1. **Fast forward:** Imagine your daughter as a teenager. Visualize a typical conflict that might arise, such as disagreements over curfews or peer influence.

2. **Empathetic response:** Picture yourself handling the situation with empathy. See yourself listening to her viewpoint without

interrupting, validating her feelings, and then calmly stating your concerns.

3. **Conflict resolution:** Visualize a constructive resolution. Perhaps you both compromise, or you help her understand the reasons behind certain rules. Picture both of you walking away from the conversation feeling respected and understood.

Exercise 2: Adult Relationship

1. **Look ahead:** Imagine your daughter as an adult. Visualize a scenario where she comes to you for advice on a significant life decision.

2. **Supportive dialogue:** See yourself as the wise, supportive father. Picture a dialogue where you offer both guidance and encouragement, allowing her the space to make her own decisions.

3. **Continued bond:** Visualize the long-term impact of your parenting—seeing her confident and self-assured, thanking you for your support and guidance throughout her life.

To make these visualizations impactful, try to incorporate them into your daily routine. Spend a few minutes each morning or evening closing your eyes and running through these scenarios. The more vividly you can imagine these interactions, the more natural and instinctive your responses will become in real life. This proactive approach will help you build and strengthen a loving, respectful, and supportive relationship with your daughter that stands the test of time.

Wrapping Up

Reflecting on your personal parenting history and recognizing the inherited patterns has opened the door to more intentional and responsive fathering. Throughout this chapter, we've tackled the delicate art of understanding the influences that shape your parenting, the significance of modeling desired behaviors, and the profound impact of adapting your approaches to nurture a thriving relationship with your daughter.

As we prepare to turn the page, we find ourselves on the threshold of a natural progression in our journey: the practice of communication with mindfulness. With the insights gained from reflecting on your parenting styles, you're ideally positioned to explore techniques that foster open, honest, and effective communication. Let's carry forward the reflections from this chapter and see how they can transform your conversations and connections with your daughter.

Chapter 4:

Building Communication Bridges With Mindfulness

As we continue our journey into mindful parenting, we will learn how integrating mindfulness and effective communication techniques can profoundly strengthen the bond between father and daughter. Building on what we've uncovered about understanding your emotions, managing stress, and shifting from reactive to mindful responses, we're now set to apply these insights to enhance your daily interactions.

Reflect on the previous chapters, where we explored emotional regulation and stress management. Remember how we discussed the transformative power of identifying and evolving your parenting style? Those steps were crucial in preparing you for what comes next: applying mindfulness in your conversations and everyday moments with your daughter.

Here, we'll explore practical, real-world applications of mindfulness and communication strategies that can help you and your daughter develop resilience and navigate digital distractions. These techniques will ensure that your interactions are not only heard but truly felt. So, let's build on the foundation we've set and move from the parent you are to the parent you aspire to be—engaged, empathetic, and ever-mindful of the cherished relationship with your daughter.

Building Resilience Through Mindful Communication

When we talk about resilience in children and teens, we're talking about their ability to bounce back from setbacks, adapt to adversity, and face life's challenges with courage and confidence. The role of effective communication, supported by mindfulness, in fostering this resilience cannot be overstated. It's the bridge that connects a father's intentions to his daughter's understanding, helping her navigate through life's turbulent waters with greater assurance.

Mindful communication starts with **presence**—a total, unadulterated focus on the moment and the person you're with. For fathers, this means engaging with your daughter without the distractions of your phone buzzing, the TV in the background, or even their mental checklist of tasks. When you are fully present, your daughter feels valued and heard, reinforcing her self-worth and empowering her to express herself openly.

But being present is just the start. Effective communication also requires **active listening** and responses that affirm your daughter's feelings and thoughts. For instance, if she's upset over a dispute with a friend, avoid jumping to quick fixes. Instead, respond with empathy: "It sounds like you're really hurt by what happened. Would you like to talk more about it?" This approach validates her feelings and encourages her to explore her emotions further, aiding the development of her emotional intelligence and resilience.

Encouraging **open dialogue** about both successes and failures is another key aspect. Celebrate her achievements without focusing solely on performance, and frame failures as opportunities for learning, not as grounds for criticism. For example, if she struggles with a test, discuss what she learned and how she can improve her study methods rather than fixating on the grade.

Building and maintaining **trust** is vital in nurturing resilience. Trust forms the core of any strong relationship. Show that you trust her judgments, respect her opinions, and support her choices, even when they differ from your own. Be consistent in your words and actions—keep promises, attend her events, and take her concerns seriously. This consistency helps her feel secure and confident in expressing her true self.

Moreover, demonstrating **vulnerability** as a father by sharing your own experiences and acknowledging your mistakes helps her see that it's okay to be imperfect. This openness deepens your connection and makes her more likely to approach you with her problems, knowing she won't be judged harshly.

Remember, by modeling mindful communication, you set a powerful example of how to manage interpersonal interactions. Daughters who observe their fathers handle challenges with calmness and clarity learn to replicate these behaviors. They learn resilience not by avoiding difficulties but by effectively dealing with them—a lesson that will serve them well throughout their lives. Mindful communication teaches daughters to see setbacks as feedback, not failures, instilling a growth mindset that fosters resilience.

Core Mindful Communication Techniques for Engaged Fatherhood

Here are some core mindfulness techniques along with practical strategies to incorporate them into daily interactions. These tools are about improving your relationship with your daughter, enriching your interactions, and ensuring you're truly connected, no matter what distractions may arise.

Active Listening

Active listening is all about fully concentrating on what is being said rather than just passively hearing the message of the speaker (Active Listening, n.d.). It involves listening with all senses. As a father, practicing active listening can transform ordinary conversations into moments of deep understanding and connection. Here's how to practice it:

- **Focus fully:** Start by giving your daughter your undivided attention. This means putting aside all distractions. When she talks, listen with the intent to understand, not to respond. This shows her that her words are valuable to you.

- **Encourage expression:** Encourage her to express herself fully, without interruption. Sometimes, all it takes is a nod or a simple "uh-huh" to signal that you're engaged. Ask open-ended questions that prompt her to elaborate on her thoughts and feelings. For example, "What was the best part of your day?" or "How did that make you feel?" These questions show that you're interested in the nuances of her experiences, not just the headlines.

- **Reflect on her feelings:** As you listen, pay close attention to the emotions behind the words. Reflect these feelings back to her to show that you understand. For instance, if she's excited about a school project, respond with enthusiasm in your voice; if she's upset, your tone can be more subdued and sympathetic. Say things like, "It sounds like you were really excited about that!" or "That must have been really disappointing for you."

- **Summarize and clarify:** After she's finished speaking, summarize or paraphrase what you've heard to ensure there's no misunderstanding. This could be as simple as, "So you're saying that you felt left out when you weren't picked for the team?" Clarifying not only ensures you're on the same page but also shows her that you genuinely care about getting her story right.

- **Respond appropriately:** Once you're sure you understand her perspective, respond appropriately. This could be with advice, if she's seeking it, or it might be with empathy and validation of her feelings. Sometimes, the best response is simply acknowledging her feelings and offering your support. Let her know that it's okay to feel how she feels and that you're there for her, no matter what.

Nonjudgmental Feedback

Giving feedback without passing judgment is crucial in maintaining an open line of communication. It helps keep the dialogue constructive, encouraging your daughter to open up about her thoughts and feelings without fear of criticism.

- **Practicing empathy:** Start with empathy. Try to see the world through her eyes. Even if you don't agree with her actions or feelings, acknowledge the validity of her experiences. Phrases like "I can see why you'd feel that way" or "That sounds like it was really tough for you" help validate her feelings. This validation is crucial for her to feel secure in sharing deeper, more complex emotions with you.

- **Practicing mirroring:** Building from empathy, this technique involves mirroring both her verbal and nonverbal communications. By subtly mirroring her body language, tone of voice, or facial expressions, you can create a sense of understanding, making her feel more connected and supported.

- **Focus on the positive:** When giving feedback, focus on the positives. Highlight her strengths and the things she did well before addressing areas where she could improve. For example, if she's dealing with a conflict at school, you might say, "I'm really proud of you for standing up for what you believe in," before discussing ways she might effectively manage the conflict next time.

- **Guide rather than direct:** Instead of dictating what she should do, guide her by asking thought-provoking questions that encourage her to consider different perspectives and solutions. Questions like "What do you think you could do differently next time?" or "How could you handle this if it happens again?" empower her to think critically and develop her problem-solving skills.

- **Offer choices:** Give her options instead of instructions. By offering choices, you're supporting her autonomy and encouraging her to take responsibility for her decisions. This practice helps build her self-esteem and decision-making skills, which are crucial for her personal development.

- **Be honest but gentle:** While it's important to be honest, it's equally important to be gentle. Frame your feedback in a way that's supportive and constructive, rather than critical. Use "I" statements to express your thoughts and feelings about the situation, which can help prevent her from feeling attacked. For example, saying "I worry when you come home late without calling" instead of "You're always irresponsible" helps keep the conversation open and free from defensiveness.

- **Use of humor:** Lightening conversations with appropriate humor can help ease tensions and make difficult discussions more bearable. Humor can be a powerful tool to break the ice and reduce anxiety, fostering a relaxed and open communication environment.

Maintaining Presence in a Digital World

In the digital age, screens often compete for our attention, sometimes diminishing the quality of our real-life interactions. This can be particularly challenging when trying to engage with your daughter, as both of you might find yourselves distracted by notifications, the allure of social media, or simply the habit of checking your devices. However, maintaining presence is key to mindful parenting.

- **Creating screen-free zones and times:** One effective strategy is to establish certain times and areas in your home as screen-free zones.

For example, making meal times or the first hour after coming home from work or school device-free can help foster deeper conversations and connections. This not only sets a routine but also builds a predictable space where both of you know you'll have each other's undivided attention.

- **Leading by example:** Children often mirror the behavior of their parents. If you regularly check your phone during conversations, your daughter might see this as acceptable behavior. Make a conscious effort to put away your devices when engaging in conversations. Showing that you value the interaction can encourage her to do the same.

- **Discussing the impact of digital media:** Engage in open discussions about how digital media affects both of you. Talk about the benefits and the drawbacks, and understand her perspective on social media and digital interactions. This can also be a platform to discuss appropriate online behavior, privacy, and safety.

- **Mindfulness breaks:** If you find your mind wandering, practice taking quick mindfulness breaks. Focus on your breathing or the sensations in your body for a minute or two to center yourself before re-engaging.

Establishing Healthy Digital Boundaries

As a father, setting boundaries around the use of digital devices and social media is part of guiding your daughter through the digital world.

- **Age-appropriate guidelines:** The appropriate boundaries for a preschooler are different from those for a teenager. For younger children, you might limit screen time to educational content or short, supervised sessions. Teenagers, on the other hand, will require more freedom but also guidance on responsibly managing their screen time and the content they engage with.

- **Negotiating screen time:** Instead of imposing strict rules, work with your daughter to set reasonable screen time limits. This can involve negotiating screen time based on daily or weekly schedules and ensuring that digital engagements do not interfere with schoolwork, sleep, and family time. It's about finding a balance that works for both of you, respecting her needs for autonomy and connection with her peers while also ensuring she engages with the world beyond her screens.

- **Educational opportunities:** Use technology as a bridge rather than a barrier. Find apps, games, and educational programs that you can explore together. This not only makes screen time interactive but also educational, and it provides a shared activity that can help strengthen your bond.

- **Regular check-ins:** Regularly revisit your agreements about screen time and digital content as your daughter grows and her world expands. Her needs and the challenges she faces will evolve, and so should your strategies for managing them. These check-ins can also serve as opportunities to discuss any new concerns or observations about how digital interactions affect her.

Nonverbal Communication

While we often focus a lot on what to say and how to say it, there's a whole world of communication happening without us even uttering a word. Nonverbal communication—those nods, smiles, and even the way we sit—plays a massive part in connecting with our daughters.

It's about more than just standing tall (though good posture never hurts). It's the open arms when she's had a tough day or the high-five when she nails something she's been working on. These gestures speak volumes. When you're chatting with your daughter, try leaning in slightly—this shows you're interested in what she has to say. But remember, leaning in too much might invade her space, so keep it balanced.

- **Eye contact:** Eye contact is another powerful tool. When she's talking, maintaining eye contact shows you're fully engaged. It tells her, "I'm listening, I'm here, and I value what you have to say." But, of course, too much eye contact can be a bit intense, so it's okay to break it now and then to keep things comfortable.

- **Reflecting and responding without words:** Have you ever noticed how a simple nod can encourage someone to keep talking? Or how a furrowed brow can signal that you're concerned or confused? These are the ways we can respond to our daughters without interrupting them. It encourages a flow in conversation that feels supportive and constructive. Physical touch can also be a comforting form of communication, whether it's a reassuring pat on the back or a comforting hug.

- **Proximity and personal space:** Understanding and respecting personal space is crucial. Every kid is different; some may treasure their personal space more than others. It's like a dance—sometimes you step in close, and other times you give her the space to come to you. Paying attention to how she responds to different distances can help you understand her comfort levels.

- **Synchronizing your signals:** Your body language must match up with what you're saying. Imagine telling your daughter you're happy while your arms are crossed and your face is stern—it sends mixed messages, right? Being consistent helps build trust and teaches her to read and respect nonverbal cues as well.

- **Practice makes perfect:** Try setting up some fun exercises at home to get better at this. You could play a game where you guess each other's emotions based on facial expressions and body language alone. It's a fun way to become more attuned to each other's nonverbal cues.

Embedding these mindfulness techniques into your daily interactions doesn't require monumental changes. Start small—perhaps with a dedicated conversation each day using these techniques—and as you and your daughter get accustomed to the rhythm, these practices will begin to feel more natural. Over time, these small shifts can dramatically enhance the quality of your relationship.

Practical Exercises and Reflections

Embarking on a journey to deepen the bond with your daughter through improved communication and mindfulness is both exciting and transformative. This section is packed with practical exercises and reflective activities designed to enhance your interaction skills and emotional connections.

Engaging in this process can be transformative but may also highlight challenging aspects of your parenting style, including negative traits explored in earlier chapters.

Being aware of these traits during role-plays and other exercises can help you recognize them more clearly in real-life interactions. This awareness is a powerful tool—it allows you to actively choose responses that align with the values and aspirations you've identified for your relationship with your daughter.

Practicing Communication Mastery: Role-Play Scenarios for Fathers and Daughters

Navigating crucial conversations and managing conflicts effectively are essential skills for any parent, especially fathers striving to build strong, resilient relationships with their daughters. Here's a set of detailed role-play scenarios designed to enhance communication skills and provide practical experience in handling real-life situations.

Scenario 1: School Performance Concerns

Situation: Your daughter has brought home a report card that is significantly below her usual standard. You want to address the issue without making her feel attacked or defensive.

Role-play:

- **Father:** Begins the conversation after dinner, in a private, quiet setting. "I noticed your grades have dipped a bit this semester. Want to talk about what's going on?"

- **Daughter:** Responds either defensively or openly about her struggles.

- **Father:** Practices active listening, then responds with empathy and support. "It sounds like you've been really overwhelmed. Let's figure out how we can tackle this together. What do you think is the biggest challenge right now?"

Objective: To open a dialogue that allows the daughter to share her experiences and challenges without fear of judgment and collaboratively work toward a solution.

Scenario 2: Negotiating Curfew

Situation: Your teenage daughter asks to extend her curfew by two hours for a special event. You are concerned about safety and the late hour.

Role-play:

- **Father:** Initiates a discussion before the event day. "I understand this event is important to you. Let's talk about the curfew so we both feel comfortable."

- **Daughter:** Explains why she wants to stay later and what it means to her.

- **Father:** Acknowledges her feelings and discusses his concerns. Uses nonjudgmental feedback. "I hear you, and I want you to have a good time. I'm just worried about safety, especially late at night. What if we agree on a time you feel is fun and I feel is safe?"

Objective: To practice negotiating and compromising, balancing the daughter's desire for independence with the father's concern for her safety.

Scenario 3: Handling Peer Influence

Situation: You've noticed your daughter is adopting behaviors and attitudes from her friends that you don't approve of, like being disrespectful or dismissive.

Role-play:

- **Father:** Chooses a calm time to bring up his observations. "Lately, I've noticed some changes in the way you've been speaking to us at home. It seems like something might be influencing you a bit. Do you want to talk about it?"

- **Daughter:** Might be defensive or open about her influences.

- **Father:** Maintains presence, showing he is fully engaged in the conversation. Offers guidance without direct criticism. "I understand that your friends are important to you, and it's natural to be influenced by people we like. But it's also important to think about how we want to treat our family and others. What are your thoughts on that?"

Objective: To encourage the daughter to reflect on her actions and their impacts, fostering self-awareness and decision-making aligned with family values.

Scenario 4: Discussing Sensitive Topics

Situation: Your daughter is starting to ask questions about sensitive topics like relationships, alcohol, or other adult issues.

Role-play:

- **Father:** Initiates a comfortable, private setting for a chat. "I've noticed you're starting to ask more adult questions, and I want you to know I'm here to talk about whatever you need."
- **Daughter:** Poses a tough question or shares a concern about what she's heard or seen.
- **Father:** Uses the opportunity to guide her through thoughtful, nonjudgmental feedback. "That's a great question, and I'm glad you brought it up. Here's what I think, and why I think this way…"

Objective: To ensure the daughter feels supported and comfortable discussing anything with her father, enhancing trust and openness.

These role-play scenarios offer you a chance to practice maintaining composure, empathy, and engagement in various parenting challenges. You can better prepare yourself to handle real-life situations with confidence and emotional intelligence by rehearsing these interactions.

Harnessing the Power of Storytelling

Storytelling is a magical tool, not just for bedtime tales but as a way to weave stronger emotional threads between you and your daughter. Think of storytelling as your secret weapon for nurturing a deep, understanding relationship. It's about sharing those little snippets from your own life, delving into tales that open up new worlds of imagination and reality, and creating a routine that brings both of you closer on an emotional level.

- **Share personal stories:** Start by sharing stories from your own life. It could be the challenges you faced growing up, a funny incident from your high school days, or an inspiring tale of how you overcame difficulties. These stories don't just entertain; they teach resilience, impart values, and give your daughter a deeper understanding of who you are. Plus, they set the stage for trust, showing her that it's okay to share her own experiences and feelings.

- **Explore mutual interests through stories:** Use storytelling to explore interests that both of you share. Whether it's a passion for outer space, love for a sport, or an interest in ancient cultures, find books, documentaries, and tales in these realms. Discuss these stories, ask questions about what she thinks and feels, and connect these narratives to real-life situations or decisions.

- **Maintain regular emotional check-ins:** Make storytelling part of your regular emotional check-ins. You can set aside a time each week when you both share stories that reflect how you've felt during the week or any emotional challenges you faced. This practice encourages openness and can help you both manage emotions better by talking them through within the safety of a narrative.

You're just keeping communication alive, enriching it with emotions, lessons, and mutual understanding that can help your daughter feel secure, valued, and connected by incorporating storytelling into your interactions.

Daily Practices for Mindful Communication and Reflective Journaling

Boosting mindful communication with your daughter isn't just a one-off effort; it's a daily commitment that grows and deepens over time. Incorporating specific daily exercises can help you stay on track and make meaningful progress in how you connect with your daughter. Here are some tailored practices to integrate into your routine:

- **Morning intentions:** Start each day by setting a clear, positive intention. Take a few moments each morning to meditate on how you want to interact with your daughter throughout the day. This could be as simple as, "Today, I will listen more than I speak," or "Today, I will show patience and understanding."

- **Breathing breaks:** Throughout the day, especially before interactions that might be stressful or emotionally charged, take a minute to engage in deep breathing exercises. This helps reset your emotional state and allows you to approach situations with calmness and clarity.

- **Evening recaps:** End the day by discussing what went well and what could have been better. This isn't just about giving advice; it's also about sharing your own experiences and vulnerabilities.

- **Milestone notes:** Make it a habit to note down significant conversations or milestones in your relationship. This could be moments when you felt particularly connected or times when a mindful approach helped resolve a conflict.

- **Feedback reflections:** Regularly review and write down any feedback your daughter gives you about how she feels regarding your interactions. This can provide invaluable insights into how effectively you are applying your skills.

These exercises are stepping stones to a richer, more understanding relationship with your daughter. Each step you take brings you closer to becoming the mindful, supportive father you aspire to be, enhancing both of your lives in profound ways.

Wrapping Up

We've uncovered powerful tools for strengthening the bond between father and daughter through mindful communication. These strategies, rooted in trust and mutual respect, set the stage for even deeper explorations.

Next, we'll learn how to nurture our child's independence. This chapter will empower you to support your daughter's autonomy and help her thrive in a world that values gender equality. Ready to learn how to be not just her hero, but her ally? Let's get started in our next exciting chapter.

Chapter 5:

Empowering Autonomy—The Feminist Father's Guide

As your daughters grow, one of your biggest goals as parents is to help them become independent and self-reliant. But what does independence really mean for young girls today? It's about more than just making decisions on their own; it's about feeling confident and secure in those decisions, understanding the importance of personal space, and navigating the world without being boxed in by gender stereotypes.

In this chapter, we'll explore the different ways you can nurture your daughter's sense of independence. We'll talk about the importance of giving her space to grow, make mistakes, and learn from them. We'll also go into the topic of gender stereotypes—those pesky expectations society might throw her way just because she's a girl—and discuss practical strategies to help her, and even ourselves, dismantle these outdated notions.

Importantly, the principles we've discussed in previous chapters, such as emotional regulation, stress management, and mindful communication, form the bedrock of fostering a strong, autonomous character.

Emotional regulation helps her understand and manage her feelings, enabling her to make thoughtful decisions even in challenging situations. Effective stress management equips her with tools to handle pressures without feeling overwhelmed, maintaining her sense of self. Mindful communication ensures she can express her needs and boundaries clearly, fostering healthy relationships and personal respect.

By the end of this chapter, you'll have a clearer understanding of how empowering your daughter with independence prepares her for the challenges of the world and supports her in becoming a strong, resilient individual. So, let's get started on this important journey together.

Understanding Independence, Interdependence, and Codependence

To truly support your daughter in her journey toward becoming strong and autonomous, it's important to understand the different concepts of independence, interdependence, and codependence. Each plays a unique role in personal development and relationships, and finding the right balance is key.

Independence

Independence is the ability to think, act, and make decisions on one's own. It involves having confidence in oneself and being able to rely on one's own personal strengths and resources. For your daughter, independence means feeling capable of tackling challenges, solving problems, and making choices without always needing to seek approval or assistance from others. It's about developing a sense of self-efficacy and trust in her own abilities.

Interdependence

Interdependence is the recognition that, while independence is valuable, humans are social creatures who thrive through mutual support and collaboration. In an interdependent relationship, individuals can rely on each other for help, share responsibilities, and work together to achieve common goals. It's a healthy balance where each person maintains their independence while also valuing and benefiting from their connections with others. Teaching your daughter interdependence means showing her how to build supportive relationships where she can give and receive help, learn from others, and contribute to her community.

Codependence

Codependence, on the other hand, is an unhealthy dynamic where one person's self-worth and identity are overly reliant on another person. In codependent relationships, individuals may have difficulty making decisions without their partner, constantly seek approval, or sacrifice their own needs to please others. This can lead to a lack of personal growth and an imbalance in the relationship. It's crucial to help your daughter understand the signs of codependence so she can avoid falling into these patterns and instead foster healthy, balanced relationships.

Balancing Independence and Interdependence

The goal is to help your daughter strike a balance between being independent and maintaining healthy, interdependent connections within the family and the broader community. Start by helping her develop skills in emotional regulation and mindful communication, as discussed in previous chapters. These skills will enable her to navigate relationships with awareness and empathy, understanding her own needs and respecting those of others. Other steps you can take include:

Modeling Healthy Relationships

Healthy relationships are built on mutual respect, trust, and open communication. Imagine a situation where you and your partner disagree about something important, like finances. Instead of arguing or shutting down, you both sit down and talk openly about your concerns and listen to each other's perspectives. By finding a compromise that respects both viewpoints, you show your daughter that conflicts can be resolved through understanding and collaboration.

Another example is how you show appreciation and respect for each other daily. Simple acts like saying "thank you" when your partner does something kind or taking the time to ask about their day demonstrate the importance of valuing one another. When your daughter sees this, she learns that healthy relationships are nurtured through everyday actions of respect and kindness.

Discussing Healthy Dependency

Healthy dependency means being able to rely on others when needed while maintaining your independence. For instance, if you're feeling overwhelmed with work or household tasks, you might ask your partner or a friend for help. This doesn't mean you can't handle things on your own; it shows that you understand the importance of support and teamwork.

Similarly, encourage your daughter to ask for help when she needs it. Whether it's with schoolwork, emotions, or friendships, let her know it's okay to lean on others. Share stories of times when you needed assistance and how accepting help made things better. This teaches her that seeking support is a strength, not a weakness.

Recognizing Unhealthy Dependency

Start by explaining what unhealthy dependency looks like. For instance, if she feels she can't make decisions without someone else's approval or constantly seeks validation from others, these are signs of unhealthy dependency. Another indicator might be if she sacrifices her own needs and well-being to please others, or if she feels anxious or insecure when not in constant contact with someone.

Share examples from everyday life. Perhaps she has a friend who always needs her to solve their problems, making her feel responsible for their happiness. Or maybe she feels she can't say no to someone, even when she really wants to. These situations can highlight how unhealthy dependency can manifest in different ways.

As a father, sharing your own experiences can profoundly impact her understanding and growth. Discuss times when you found yourself in unhealthy relationship dynamics. Explain how being in a codependent relationship made you feel—perhaps you felt like you couldn't be happy unless the other person was, or you ignored your own needs to maintain peace in the relationship.

Talk about the emotional and psychological effects these dynamics had on you and possibly the other partner. For example, you might have felt a constant strain or dissatisfaction or noticed that it stunted your personal growth. Explain the realizations that led you to recognize these patterns as problematic.

Most importantly, discuss how you resolved these issues and what you learned from your experiences. Maybe you sought help through counseling, read insightful books, or took time for self-reflection to understand your tendencies toward codependency. Share how these actions helped you establish healthier boundaries and develop a stronger sense of self-worth.

Encouraging Self-Reliance

To encourage her to seek balance, start by promoting the idea of self-reliance. Self-reliance is the bridge between independence and interdependence. It's about trusting her own abilities and judgment while knowing when and how to lean on others for support.

Help her understand that it's okay to rely on others but equally important to trust herself. Encourage her to make decisions on her own and support her in learning from any mistakes. This builds her confidence and helps her see that she can handle things independently.

For instance, if she's working on a school project, let her take the lead in planning and execution, offering guidance only when she asks for it. Celebrate her successes and discuss what she learned from any challenges she faced. This approach reinforces her ability to trust her own judgment and problem-solving skills.

Shifting from a controlling to a curious and caring approach in parenting is crucial for fostering a nurturing environment. This shift means moving from directing her actions to understanding and supporting her choices. When your daughter knows that you're there to listen and support rather than control, she feels more secure in exploring her own capabilities.

Setting Boundaries

Discuss the importance of setting boundaries. Explain that boundaries are like invisible lines that protect our personal space and well-being. They help us define what we are comfortable with and what we aren't. Make sure she knows that it's okay to set limits with friends, family, and even with you.

You can use role-playing to practice setting boundaries. For example, act out a scenario where a friend asks her to do something she's not comfortable with. Help her find polite but firm ways to say no, like, "I'm sorry, but I can't help with that right now," or "I need some time for myself today." Role-playing helps her feel more prepared and confident to handle real-life situations.

Respecting and Promoting Personal Space and Solitude

Alongside setting boundaries, it's crucial to respect and promote your daughter's need for solitude and personal space. This is vital for self-reflection, peace of mind, and developing inner strength without external influences. Encourage her to take time for herself to relax, think, and recharge.

This self-reflection helps her understand herself better, recognize her strengths and weaknesses, and make thoughtful decisions. Encourage her to keep a journal where she can write about her day, her feelings, and her dreams. This practice can be a powerful tool for self-discovery and personal growth.

If she enjoys reading, drawing, or just sitting quietly in her room, make sure she knows it's okay to spend time alone. Let her know that you support her need for personal space and that it's a healthy part of life. Share with her how you take time for yourself and how it helps you feel more balanced and ready to face challenges.

For example, if she feels overwhelmed by social activities, she can say something like, "I love spending time with you, but I need some time alone to recharge." This way, she maintains her relationships while also honoring her own needs.

Confronting and Dismantling Gender Stereotypes

Understanding the unique ways your children grow and perceive the world can profoundly shape how you support and guide them as they develop their identities and independence. It's essential, especially for daughters, to recognize the roles both biology and society play in shaping their experiences.

Firstly, we need to appreciate that while males and females share many similarities, they are biologically different in ways that matter, especially in brain structure and function. Research has shown that these differences are not just anatomical but also influence cognitive abilities and behavioral patterns from a very young age. For example, studies have indicated that even in early childhood, boys and girls may show different preferences and abilities in toy selection and play styles, influenced by both biological factors like prenatal testosterone and societal expectations (Szadvári et al., 2023).

However, as fathers, it's important to question and challenge the rigid stereotypes that often confine your daughter to predefined roles. While biology provides a framework, it doesn't dictate destiny. Girls can excel in areas traditionally dominated by boys, such as math and science, and they should be encouraged to explore and develop skills in all areas of interest.

Additionally, gender stereotypes about emotional expression and social behaviors can limit your daughter's potential. For instance, society often encourages girls to be more empathetic and socially aware, skills that are valuable but should not be seen as their sole domain. Boys, too, benefit from developing these emotional and social skills, which are critical for personal and professional success.

Promoting Media Literacy

Media plays a significant role in shaping gender roles and stereotypes. Encouraging media literacy helps your daughter critically analyze the messages she receives from TV shows, movies, advertisements, and social media. According to Santoniccolo et al. (2023), media representations significantly influence sociocultural pressures and perceptions about gender.

Despite advances in civil rights, restrictive gender-based representations are still widely seen in various settings—like in movies, on TV shows, in advertisements, and on social media platforms—continuously reinforcing stereotypes and shaping public attitudes and behaviors.

The research underscores that media frequently perpetuates stereotypes and sexualizing depictions that support traditional gender roles and norms. Such portrayals reinforce gender-based stereotypes and have wider consequences, including encouraging sexism, harassment, and violence, especially among men, and dampening career ambitions in women. Additionally, these portrayals contribute to the acceptance of societal beauty standards, fostering sexist attitudes, tolerance of abuse, and body shaming.

For example, the study points out that ongoing exposure to stereotyped and sexualized media content can result in several harmful impacts on physical and psychological health, such as eating disorders, heightened body monitoring, and diminished body image and overall quality of life. This points to the critical need for fostering media literacy to enable young viewers, like your daughter, to recognize and critically evaluate these portrayals.

Practical Exercises and Reflections

Encouraging Decision-Making and Responsibility

This exercise involves a week-long routine where each day, your daughter gets to make certain decisions that affect not just her but the whole family. This will help her practice decision-making in a safe environment where the stakes are low but meaningful.

1. **Setup a decision calendar:** Create a simple weekly calendar that includes one decision for each day. These decisions should vary in complexity based on your daughter's age. For younger children, decisions might be about

choosing the day's breakfast or selecting a family game for the evening. Older children might decide on the weekly menu or how to spend a family day out.

2. **Daily briefing:** Each morning, have a quick chat with your daughter about the decision she needs to make for the day. Explain any factors she might need to consider. For example, if she's deciding on the dinner menu, talk about the ingredients you already have or need to buy.

3. **Research and resources:** Provide resources she might need to make informed decisions. For the dinner menu, this could be access to recipes online or in cookbooks. When deciding on a family activity, you might let her know the weather forecast or give her a list of possible nearby events.

4. **Making the decision:** Encourage her to think aloud about her choices, asking questions like, "What are the pros and cons of this option?" or "Who will be affected by this decision?" Allow her to make the final call and discuss how her decision will be implemented.

5. **Reflection:** At the end of the day, spend a few minutes discussing how her decision turned out. Was it effective? Did anything unexpected happen? This reflection will help her learn from the experience and improve her decision-making skills over time.

6. **Weekly review:** At the end of the week, have a longer discussion about all the decisions made throughout the week. Discuss what went well and what could be improved. This reinforces the learning and highlights the importance of decision-making in everyday life.

Example Scenario for a Week

- **Monday:** Choose what to pack for lunch.
- **Tuesday:** Decide the family's evening activity (movie night, board games, etc.).
- **Wednesday:** Plan the outfit for a family outing on the weekend.
- **Thursday:** Select a new book to read together as a family.
- **Friday:** Choose the dinner menu for Saturday night.
- **Saturday:** Decide on a weekend activity (visit a museum, go to a park, etc.).
- **Sunday:** Reflect on the week's decisions and prepare for the upcoming week.

This exercise gives your daughter the chance to practice making decisions in a real-world context, which builds her confidence and critical thinking skills. She learns about responsibility and the impact of her decisions by reflecting on her choices and seeing the outcomes. Moreover, involving her in daily family decisions reinforces her role and value within the family unit, boosting her self-esteem and sense of belonging.

Supporting Your Daughter's Unique Interests and Strengths

This activity is designed to be an ongoing dialogue between you and your daughter, focusing on exploring and supporting her interests and strengths. It's structured around regular "Interest Exploration Days" that you and your daughter will plan and execute together.

1. **Set up an interest exploration day:** Schedule a day each month dedicated to exploring a new activity or subject of your daughter's choosing. This could be anything from a science workshop, a sports clinic, an art class, or a visit to a local museum or library.

2. **Planning together:** Sit down with your daughter to plan the day. Discuss what she's interested in trying out or learning more about. If she's unsure, help her brainstorm based on what she enjoys at school or at home.

3. **Research and resources:** Together, look up information about the activity. If it's a sport, watch some videos of it being played. If it's an art form, look at examples online or in books.

This preparation will make the exploration day more engaging.

4. **Engagement:** Participate in the activity with your daughter or be there to support her as she engages in it. This shows that you value her interests and are willing to invest your time in them as well.

5. **Reflective discussion:** After the activity, ask questions like:

    - "What did you enjoy most about today?"
    - "Is this something you'd like to learn more about or continue doing?"
    - "How did trying something new make you feel?"

6. **Father's reflective journal:** After several exploration days, spend some time reflecting on your own thoughts about the activities. Consider questions such as:

    - "How well do I feel I am supporting my daughter's exploration and independence?"
    - "What can I do to better encourage her individuality and confidence?"
    - "In what ways have I noticed her growing through these activities?"

Example of an Interest Exploration Day

1. **Preparation:** Your daughter expresses interest in robotics. Together, you find a local workshop or an online tutorial series on beginner robotics.

2. **Activity day:** You attend the workshop together or gather materials and follow an online tutorial at home.

3. **Discussion:** Discuss what parts of robotics she found most intriguing and whether she'd like to participate in a robotics club or school team.

By regularly engaging with your daughter in new activities, you show that her interests are important and worth investing in. This boosts her confidence to try new things and helps her discover her passions and strengths. Your involvement also reinforces the message that she has your support in whatever path she chooses to pursue, which is crucial for developing her independence and self-assurance.

A Collaborative Approach to Encouraging Your Daughter's Lifestyle Choices

Besides participating in Interest Exploration Days, there are many other strategies you can use to actively support and encourage your daughter:

- **Shared activities:** Participate in activities that your daughter enjoys or wants to try. Whether it's a sport, an art class, or a science project, being involved shows that you value her interests and are willing to invest your time in them.

- **Goal setting together:** Help your daughter set realistic goals related to her interests. Teach her how to break down these goals into manageable steps and celebrate small achievements along the way to keep her motivated.

- **Educational support:** Support her educational pursuits by providing resources for learning more about her areas of interest. This might involve books, online courses, tutoring, or visits to museums and educational workshops.

- **Role modeling:** Open up about your own challenges and how you've managed them. Whether it's a tough project at work, a personal goal you struggled to achieve, or how you balance your time between hobbies and family duties, share the lessons you learned. This doesn't just show her the decisions you made but also the values and priorities that guided those decisions.

- **Discussing role models:** Introduce her to diverse role models who can inspire her. Discuss the qualities and achievements of successful people in her areas of interest, especially other women who can serve as powerful examples of what she can aspire to achieve.

- **Supporting social interactions:** Encourage her to interact with peers who share her interests, whether it's through clubs, teams, or social groups. Peer support can be motivational and enhance her learning and enjoyment in these areas.

- **Creating a supportive environment:** Create a home environment that supports her learning and interests. This might mean designated spaces for studying or practicing a hobby, or simply a home atmosphere that values and respects her choices and personal development.

- **Reshape narratives together:** If she faces setbacks or challenges, listen to how she describes and reacts to them. Help her reshape any negative narratives into empowering ones. For example, if she says, "I'm terrible at math," you could help her reframe it to, "Math is challenging for me, so I need to practice more and maybe get some help." This teaches her resilience and the power of a positive mindset.

Remember to encourage her to make her own decisions where appropriate to foster independence and critical thinking. By using these strategies, you can play a pivotal role in helping your daughter develop a strong sense of self, confidence in her abilities, and an independent spirit that will serve her well throughout her life.

Wrapping Up

Empowering your daughter with independence is a fundamental step toward preparing her for the broader challenges of life. By instilling confidence, teaching her to navigate gender stereotypes, and nurturing her emotional regulation and communication skills, you're setting a foundation for her to grow into a resilient and self-assured individual. This journey of fostering independence supports her personal growth and strengthens your bond with her as she learns to trust her capabilities and values the support and guidance you provide.

However, life often presents challenges that can disrupt even the best groundwork, such as experiences of trauma. The next chapter will explore understanding, managing, and supporting your daughter through such difficulties. We'll learn effective communication and therapeutic strategies to create a safe, nurturing environment that fosters healing and builds resilience, ensuring she can recover and grow from these experiences. Join me as we learn how to become a pivotal support system in your daughter's life during her most vulnerable times.

Chapter 6:

Supportive Strategies for Managing Trauma

While you are loving and nurturing your daughter in the best ways possible, there may come a time when life throws a curveball. It's not something anyone wishes for, but sometimes trauma can touch our lives, and when it does, the role you play in your daughter's life becomes even more crucial.

Understanding trauma, managing its impacts, and supporting your daughter through her healing process are fundamental. This chapter is dedicated to guiding you on how to be there for her during possibly one of the toughest times she might face. Whether it's a result of an accident, loss, bullying, or any distressing event, the way you respond can make a profound difference in her journey to recovery.

Trauma can shake the very foundation of our sense of safety and normalcy. For a young girl, this disruption can be particularly disorienting. As her father, your support can become her anchor, providing stability when everything else seems unpredictable. Effective communication is your strongest tool here. It's about listening—truly listening—with an open heart and mind, acknowledging her feelings without judgment, and validating her experiences. This alone can be incredibly healing.

In this chapter, we'll explore some therapeutic strategies that you can use to create a nurturing and safe environment for your daughter. These are not just clinical approaches but also simple, everyday actions that reinforce your love and commitment to her well-being. From maintaining routines that provide comfort and security to encouraging expressions through art or music, we'll cover a range of practices that promote healing and resilience.

Your role is pivotal. It's about being present, being patient, and being a source of unconditional love. Let's discover how you can strengthen your bond with your daughter and equip her with the resilience to overcome life's challenges.

Recognizing the Signs: Understanding Trauma in Your Daughter

Before you can support your daughter through trauma, it's crucial to understand what trauma is and how it might manifest in her life. Trauma is an emotional reaction to an extremely upsetting or shocking event that surpasses an individual's capacity to manage, triggers a sense of powerlessness, reduces their self-esteem, and restricts their ability to experience a range of emotions and life events fully (Schroeder et al., 2021). It's not the actual circumstances that decide if an event is traumatic, but rather an individual's personal emotional response to the event. The same event might be more traumatic for one person than for another.

The impact of trauma can vary widely depending on your daughter's age and developmental stage. Younger children might not have the words to describe their feelings or what happened to them, making it harder for them to seek help. Adolescents, dealing with the normal stresses of teenage life, might hide their feelings for fear of standing out or not being understood. Each stage requires a different approach from you, with a common thread being your unwavering support and understanding.

Here's a comprehensive list of signs that might indicate your daughter is experiencing trauma. These signs are grouped into three categories: emotional, physical, and behavioral.

Emotional Signs

- **Increased anxiety or fear:** She might appear more nervous than usual, have trouble sleeping, or express fears about things that didn't seem to bother her before.

- **Mood swings or emotional instability:** Watch for sudden bursts of anger, intense irritability, or periods of unexplained crying.

- **Withdrawal:** She may pull away from family or friends, spending much more time alone.

- **Confusion or difficulty concentrating:** You might notice she seems more distracted or has trouble focusing on tasks she used to handle easily.

Physical Signs

- **Changes in eating habits:** This could be eating significantly more or less than usual.

- **Unexplained aches and pains:** Complaints about stomach aches, headaches, or other physical pains without a clear cause could be a sign.

- **Easily startled:** A heightened startle response is common among those who have experienced trauma.

- **Changes in sleeping patterns:** This includes trouble falling or staying asleep, nightmares, or sleeping more than usual.

Behavioral Signs

- **Regressing to earlier behaviors:** Younger children might start bed-wetting, thumb-sucking, or clinging to you more than usual.

- **Avoidance of certain places or activities:** She might suddenly refuse to go to certain places or participate in activities she used to enjoy, especially if they remind her of the traumatic event.

- **Decline in school performance:** A noticeable drop in grades or school participation can be a red flag.

- **Substance use or other risky behaviors:** This is more common in teenagers, as they might use alcohol, drugs, or engage in risky behaviors to cope with their pain.

Recognizing these signs is the first step in helping your daughter. It's important to approach her openly and without judgment, letting her know you're there for her, ready to listen and help her through whatever she's facing. In the next sections, we'll explore how to communicate effectively and provide the support she needs to heal and grow stronger.

The Neurological Response to Trauma

When trauma occurs, it activates the brain's emergency systems, particularly the amygdala, which we discussed earlier as a key player in emotional processing. The amygdala signals that there is a threat, leading to a cascade of physiological responses designed to protect her—the fight-or-flight response. This is useful in immediate, short-term situations, but when the threat is emotional or there's no physical escape possible, it can become problematic.

This heightened state of alert causes significant changes in other brain areas, too, such as the hippocampus and the prefrontal cortex. The hippocampus is crucial for forming new memories and retrieving old ones. Under continuous stress from trauma, its ability to function can diminish, leading to difficulties in learning and memory retention. The prefrontal cortex, responsible for decision-making, reasoning, and behavioral control, also gets less blood flow and fewer neural connections during high-stress responses (Peverill et al., 2023). This can result in impaired judgment and decision-making, making it hard for your daughter to manage her reactions and emotions effectively.

Emotional and Physiological Changes

Traumatically induced changes in brain function can lead to a range of emotional and physiological symptoms. On the emotional side, you might notice increased anxiety, persistent sadness, or emotional numbness. These are signs that her brain is trying to protect her from further emotional pain by dulling the response to emotional stimuli.

Physiologically, trauma can lead to altered stress hormone levels, such as cortisol, which can affect everything from her immune system to her energy levels. This might manifest as fatigue, changes in appetite, or a new sensitivity to physical illnesses. Such dysregulation can contribute to both heightened negative reactions to distressing experiences and a general vulnerability to mental health issues (Aas et al., 2020).

The Cycle of Reactivity and Withdrawal

The interaction between the amygdala, hippocampus, and prefrontal cortex can create a cycle of reactivity and withdrawal. This means that your daughter might swing between being overly reactive to minor triggers—because her amygdala is in overdrive—and withdrawing or shutting down as her prefrontal cortex fails to engage properly. Understanding this cycle can help you recognize when she is struggling to process trauma and needs support.

Bridging the Gap With Mindful Support

Knowing how trauma affects the brain informs how you can effectively support your daughter. It's about understanding the underlying causes. By revisiting our discussions on stress management, emotional regulation, and communication, you can see how these strategies are not just good parenting practices; they are essential tools for helping her navigate the aftermath of trauma.

Creating a supportive and safe environment is crucial in this journey. As a parent, your role is to foster a space where open communication and trust can flourish. This involves being there for her, not just physically but emotionally and mentally as well. Make sure to maintain eye contact when she speaks, showing that you are fully present and engaged. Choose your words carefully to ensure they convey understanding and support.

Your daughter needs to know that it's okay to express her feelings, whatever they may be, without fear of judgment or dismissal. Show care and nurturing in your responses, reinforcing that her emotions are valid and important. This supportive presence will help her feel secure and valued, making it easier for her to open up about her thoughts and experiences.

Remember, after experiencing trauma, your daughter may feel isolated or misunderstood. She might worry that her feelings are too much for others to handle or that expressing them might cause discomfort or upset her loved ones. It's your job to reassure her that her feelings are valid and that you are there to listen and support her, not to solve everything immediately. This reassurance can make all the difference in how she copes and recovers.

Trust is another cornerstone of this supportive environment. This isn't built overnight but is cultivated through consistent, patient, and understanding interactions. Show her that you're reliable, that you keep your promises, and that you will always take her concerns seriously. When she sees that she can trust you with her smallest worries, she'll feel more secure coming to you with the bigger ones.

Going through this together also means sometimes just being there, offering a hug, or sitting quietly with her. Your presence alone can be a powerful reassurance that she's not alone, that she's safe, and that she's loved, no matter what.

However, it's also important for you to recognize that you are not alone in this journey either. Don't hesitate to reach out for support when you need it. This could be from other family members, friends, or professionals. Seeking help sets a positive example for managing difficult emotions and ensures that you are emotionally and mentally prepared to provide the best support for your daughter. Your well-being is just as crucial in this healing process, and taking care of yourself is key to taking care of each other.

Seeking Professional Help: Navigating Therapeutic Options for Trauma Recovery

Recognizing when to seek professional help for your daughter's trauma response is crucial. It's a significant step in the recovery process, one that underscores your commitment to her healing. Professional therapy can provide specialized tools and support that extend beyond what even the most caring and dedicated parent can offer on their own. Here, we'll explore several therapeutic interventions and guide you on how to find the right professional support for your daughter.

- **Cognitive-behavioral therapy (CBT):** This type of therapy is often at the forefront of treating trauma. CBT helps patients manage their problems by changing the way they think and behave. It's especially effective for trauma because it addresses patterns of thinking that are maladaptive and the behaviors that stem from them. Specifically, trauma-focused CBT (TF-CBT) is designed to address the unique challenges of PTSD and trauma-related disorders (Murray et al., 2022). While CBT mainly focuses on thoughts and behaviors, it is often used alongside other treatments to address physical symptoms like muscle memory. For a young girl dealing with trauma, CBT can help reframe her distressing thoughts and promote healthier reactions to memories or triggers.

- **Eye movement desensitization and reprocessing (EMDR):** EMDR is another successful therapy for trauma that involves the patient remembering distressing images while undergoing various forms of bilateral sensory input, such as lateral eye movements or hand tapping. This approach is believed to aid in the processing of traumatic memories (Gainer et al., 2020).

- **Somatic experiencing:** Developed to relieve the symptoms of trauma and other mental and physical health issues, somatic experiencing focuses on the body's response to traumatic events. It's a body-oriented approach that helps release pent-up tension and energy held in the body post-trauma (Salamon, 2023). For your daughter, this could mean becoming more attuned to her physical sensations and developing strategies to manage them, which can be particularly helpful in cases where trauma manifests physically.

- **Internal family systems (IFS):** IFS is a transformative approach that recognizes and addresses multiple sub-personalities or parts within each person. These parts may carry painful emotions or traumatic memories. IFS helps patients access these parts, understand their roles, and heal them, allowing the individual to become more integrated and whole (Hodgdon et al., 2021). This approach can be particularly powerful in addressing deep-seated emotional issues and promoting self-awareness and healing.

- **Family therapy:** Since trauma affects not just the individual but also their family, this therapy includes family members in the sessions. It can be invaluable in teaching you and other family members how to best support your daughter, fostering a home environment that aids her recovery. Family therapy strengthens communication and ensures that everyone understands the roles they play in her healing journey.

- **Play therapy:** Particularly for younger children who might not have the words to express their feelings, play therapy can be a gentle yet profound way of processing trauma. Through play, therapists can help children explore their emotions and experiences in a safe environment.

- **Art therapy:** Like play therapy, art therapy offers a nonverbal outlet for expressing difficult emotions. It can be particularly effective for daughters who naturally gravitate toward drawing, painting, or crafting, providing them with a creative and therapeutic way to express their feelings and process their experiences.

- **Animal-assisted therapy:** Interaction with animals can help reduce anxiety and improve mood. Programs involving horses, dogs, or other animals can be particularly engaging for children and teens, providing comfort and a nonjudgmental space to work through emotions.

- **Pharmacotherapy:** In some cases, medication may be used as part of the treatment plan for trauma, especially when there are co-occurring issues like severe anxiety or depression. This should always be managed by a healthcare professional with experience in pediatric mental health.

Finding the Right Professional

Choosing the right therapist for your daughter involves a few steps:

- **Research:** Look into therapists' specialties and ensure they have experience dealing with children and trauma. Resources like the American Psychological Association (APA) or local mental health organizations can be useful starting points.

- **Consultation:** Many therapists offer a preliminary consultation, which can be a good opportunity to gauge how they interact with your daughter and discuss their approach to trauma therapy.

- **Check credentials:** Ensure that the therapist is licensed and registered with relevant professional bodies. This guarantees that they meet professional standards and adhere to a code of ethics.

- **Comfort and compatibility:** It's crucial that your daughter feels comfortable and safe with the therapist. Trust your instincts; if it doesn't feel right, it's okay to look for someone else who might be a better fit.

Each child's or teen's path to recovery will be unique, and often a combination of these therapies will be the most effective approach. Seeking professional help is a proactive step in supporting your daughter's recovery from trauma. While it may feel daunting at first, finding the right therapeutic support can significantly ease her healing process, helping her regain confidence and peace.

Everyday Support Strategies: Helping Your Daughter Through Trauma

As a father, your role in your daughter's recovery from trauma is invaluable. By revisiting the techniques we've already discussed, such as mindful communication, you can help recalibrate her stress responses, offering a sense of safety and stability that her brain is struggling to provide on its own. This approach does more than just soothe her symptoms; it supports her brain in rewiring itself, building new, healthier pathways. Other strategies might include:

Establishing Supportive Boundaries

Creating a safe and supportive environment starts with clear boundaries. This means giving her space when she needs it and being available when she seeks support. Respect her privacy, and let her know that her personal space is hers to control. Encourage her to express when she feels overwhelmed or needs a break from discussions about her experiences or feelings. This respects her boundaries and teaches her to recognize and communicate her needs—a crucial skill in recovery.

Empowering Through Autonomy and Self-Advocacy

Empowering your daughter involves supporting her autonomy, especially in critical areas such as her interactions with healthcare professionals. Encourage her to ask questions and express her concerns during appointments. You can practice these conversations at home by role-playing scenarios where she might need to advocate for herself. This preparation can make her feel more confident in real-life situations, knowing she has the skills to speak up for herself.

When attending appointments with her, let her take the lead as much as possible. This shows that you trust her to manage her interactions and that you're there to support her, not to control her. These small steps reinforce her sense of control over her life, an essential aspect of healing from trauma.

Building Resilience and Managing Stress

Building resilience in your daughter involves equipping her with strategies to manage stress and recover from setbacks. Revisit our earlier discussions on coping skills and mindfulness and integrate these techniques into daily life. Regular practice can help her develop a routine that fosters resilience.

- **Mindfulness and meditation:** Teach her simple mindfulness exercises that she can do daily, such as breathing techniques or guided meditations. These practices help center her thoughts and reduce feelings of anxiety or being overwhelmed.

- **Routine Exercise:** Regular physical activity, such as walking, swimming, or cycling, boosts endorphins and helps manage symptoms of depression and anxiety. Encourage her to find an activity she enjoys, which can also help in building a supportive community of peers.

- **Yoga:** While engaging in physical activities together, try yoga, which is excellent for regulating the body's stress responses and improving mental health. Yoga combines physical poses with mindful breathing and meditation, enhancing both physical and emotional strength.

- **Nutritional support:** Diet plays a significant role in mental health. Encourage a balanced diet rich in vegetables, fruits, proteins, and whole grains, which provide the necessary nutrients for brain health and overall well-being. Omega-3 fatty acids, found in fish like salmon and in flaxseeds, are particularly good for brain health. Avoiding excessive caffeine and sugar can also help stabilize mood swings and improve overall energy levels (Crichton-Stuart, 2023).

- **Encouraging social interaction:** Encourage her to maintain friendships and social activities, even if it's just small gatherings or online interactions with peers. Social support is crucial for mental health and can provide a sense of normalcy and escape from her troubles.

Structured Routines

Routines create a predictable environment that can make your daughter feel safer and more secure. Knowing what to expect each day helps reduce anxiety about the unknown, which is especially important after experiencing trauma. The certainty of a routine provides a comforting structure that supports her during uncertain times. Here are other ways establishing a structured routine can benefit your daughter:

- **Strengthened coping skills:** Regular schedules reinforce coping skills by integrating therapeutic activities and necessary breaks. For example, you might include time for relaxation techniques, such as deep breathing or mindfulness meditation, right after school or before bedtime. These activities become habits that can help manage stress and emotional spikes.

- **Improved sleep patterns:** Trauma can disrupt sleep patterns, leading to insomnia or irregular sleep schedules. A consistent bedtime routine can signal to her body that it's time to wind down and rest, improving sleep quality. This could involve quiet activities before bed, such as reading or listening to soothing music, which help transition her into sleep.

- **Enhanced focus and organization:** Structured routines can also improve concentration and organizational skills. When your daughter knows her schedule and what's expected of her, she can focus better on the task at hand. This can be particularly helpful for schoolwork and other activities that require sustained attention.

- **Emotional regulation:** By maintaining a routine, your daughter learns to anticipate and prepare for various activities, which can help her regulate her emotions. Regular exposure to manageable doses of stress, like completing a homework assignment or attending a social event, can teach her to handle stress more effectively.

- **Encouraging independence:** As your daughter grows accustomed to her routine, she can start taking more responsibility for managing her own time and activities. This fosters independence and confidence, showing her that she has control over her life and her recovery.

- **Building family bonds:** Shared routines, such as family meals or weekend outings, can strengthen family ties and provide regular opportunities for family members to check in with each other. These moments are crucial for maintaining open lines of communication and for your daughter to feel supported by her family.

By incorporating these strategies, you are not just helping your daughter heal from trauma; you are strengthening your relationship with her and building her skills for managing future challenges. Your support and understanding during this time are key components of her recovery and will empower her to emerge stronger and more resilient.

Support for Fathers: Taking Care of Yourself to Take Care of Her

Being a steady source of strength for your daughter is vital, but you can't pour from an empty cup. Taking care of your own emotional and physical well-being is not just good for you; it's essential for maintaining your ability to be there for her.

- **Recognizing your emotional load:** First, recognize that it's normal to feel overwhelmed, anxious, or even helpless at times. Witnessing your daughter struggle with trauma can be heart-wrenching, and it's okay to admit that this affects you deeply. Acknowledging your feelings doesn't make you weak; it makes you human.

- **Creating space for your own care:** Make sure to carve out time for yourself. Engage in activities that rejuvenate and fulfill you, whether that's pursuing a hobby, exercising, reading, or spending time with friends. These aren't just breaks from your responsibilities; they're crucial for recharging your mental and emotional batteries.

- **Seeking support when needed:** Don't hesitate to seek support for yourself. This could mean talking to a therapist or counselor, joining a support group for parents, or simply opening up to friends and family about what you're going through. Sharing your load doesn't mean you're burdening others; it means you're wise enough to know that everyone sometimes needs help.

- **Staying physically healthy:** Taking care of your physical health is as important as managing your emotional health. Regular exercise, a nutritious diet, and adequate sleep all contribute to your physical well-being, which in turn affects your mental and emotional resilience. When you're physically healthy, you're better equipped to handle stress and be the supportive father your daughter needs.

- **Setting your boundaries:** Learn to set boundaries, both at work and in personal relationships. It's okay to say no or to delegate tasks when needed. Setting boundaries helps prevent burnout and ensures you have the energy and patience required to support your daughter effectively.

Taking care of yourself is a central part of being a supportive parent. You're setting a strong foundation for your daughter's recovery and showing her that it's important to look after oneself, even in tough times. Remember, self-care isn't selfish—it's essential.

Practical Exercises and Reflections

As you support your daughter through her trauma recovery, engaging in practical exercises and reflections can deepen your understanding and enhance your ability to provide support. These activities are opportunities to connect, learn, and grow together. Here are some guided exercises and reflections to incorporate into your journey of supporting your daughter.

Exercise 1: Daily Check-In Journal

- **Purpose:** To foster communication and allow your daughter to express her feelings in a safe, structured way.
- **How to do it:**
    - Create a simple journal that your daughter can write in. Encourage her to jot down how she's feeling each day, what's on her mind, or anything she'd like to share.

- Decide together whether she'd like to share her entries with you. If she does, take the time to read her entries and discuss them calmly. If she prefers to keep them private, respect her choice—it's about giving her control.

- **Reflection:** Reflect on how this journal might be helping her. Ask yourself, "Is there more she wants to express verbally after writing? How can I make our discussions more open and supportive?"

Exercise 2: Father-Daughter Journaling

- **Purpose:** To enhance communication and understanding through shared journaling.

- **How to do it:**

    - Introduce the idea of having two journals—one for you and one for your daughter. These journals can serve as a space for each of you to express thoughts, feelings, and daily experiences. The themes of the journals can slightly differ to reflect individual perspectives; your daughter's journal might focus on her feelings and daily encounters, while yours might center on reflections about your interactions and ways to support her healing.

- You can choose to share your entries with each other regularly or keep some entries private. The key is to build trust and show that you are both working through this process together.

- **Reflection:** Consider the impact of this joint journaling activity on your relationship. Reflect on how sharing your thoughts and reading about her experiences may change the way you communicate and support each other. Think about whether this method allows for new insights into each other's thoughts and feelings and how it may be improving your daughter's comfort in expressing herself.

Exercise 3: Role-Playing Scenarios

- **Purpose:** To prepare your daughter to advocate for herself in various situations, such as at school or in healthcare settings.

- **How to do it:**

  - Create scenarios that she might find challenging, like speaking to a teacher about a concern or asking a doctor questions.

  - Take turns playing different roles. Allow her to practice standing up for herself while you play the supportive bystander or the other party in the scenario.

- **Reflection:** After each role-play, discuss how it felt for her. What did she do well? What would she like to improve? Reflect on how you can support her to feel more confident in real-life situations.

Exercise 4: Stress Management Techniques

- **Purpose:** To teach and practice effective stress management strategies.

- **How to do it:**

    - Together, learn about different stress management techniques such as deep breathing, progressive muscle relaxation, or mindfulness meditation.

    - For example, **deep breathing** is a simple and powerful way to reduce stress. Sit or lie down in a comfortable position. Close your eyes and focus solely on your breathing. Inhale slowly through your nose, allowing your chest and lower belly to rise as you fill your lungs. Let your abdomen expand fully. Then exhale slowly through your mouth or nose, whichever feels more comfortable. Repeat this deep breathing for several minutes, focusing on breathing deeply and slowly.

- **Progressive muscle relaxation** involves tensing and then relaxing different muscle groups in the body. Start at your toes and work your way up to your head. Tense each muscle group for about 5 seconds, and then relax for 30 seconds. Notice the sensation of release as you relax each muscle. This can be particularly helpful before bedtime to alleviate tension.

- To practice **mindfulness meditation**, sit in a quiet place with minimal distractions. Close your eyes and pay attention to your breathing without trying to change it. Notice each inhale and exhale. When your mind wanders, gently bring your focus back to your breath. Start with a few minutes and gradually increase the duration as you feel more comfortable.

- Set aside a few minutes each day to practice one of these techniques together. Make it a routine part of your day, perhaps in the morning or before bedtime.

- **Reflection:** Reflect on how these practices affect her stress levels. Consider keeping a log of her stress levels before and after the exercises to see which techniques work best.

Exercise 5: The Strengths Timeline

- **Purpose:** To help your daughter recognize her own strengths and how she has used them in the past, which can empower her in her recovery.
- **How to do it:**
  - Together, create a timeline of her life with markers for challenging times she has overcome.
  - Discuss what strengths she used to navigate those challenges. For example, was she resilient? Did she seek help when needed? How did she cope?
- **Reflection:** Reflect on this timeline whenever she feels overwhelmed or hopeless. Remind her of her strengths and discuss how she can apply them to current challenges.

Exercise 6: Setting Healthy Boundaries

- **Purpose:** To help your daughter understand and establish her own boundaries, reinforcing her sense of control and safety.

- **How to do it:**
  - Discuss what boundaries are and why they're important, especially in relationships and interactions.
  - Have her list out areas where she feels her boundaries need reinforcement, and role-play how to assert these boundaries effectively.
- **Reflection:** Reflect together on these exercises periodically. Are the boundaries being respected? How does it make her feel? What adjustments need to be made?

These exercises are designed to be interactive and evolving, based on your daughter's needs and responses. They are tools to help her manage and recover from trauma and to strengthen the bond between you.

Wrapping Up

Through this chapter, we've explored the deep and tender process of supporting your daughter through trauma. This journey, filled with its challenges and learning experiences, underscores how crucial your role is as her father. Your understanding, patience, and unwavering support are the anchors she relies on to navigate through this turbulent phase. Remember, your ability to listen deeply, acknowledge her feelings without judgment, and validate her experiences can significantly ease her path to healing.

Looking ahead, our next chapter will broaden the scope of support. We'll cover essential topics like basic self-care, menstrual health, and navigating dating and relationships. These areas are crucial to her overall well-being and require thoughtful guidance from you. So, let's expand your knowledge and skills to ensure you provide the best support for every aspect of your daughter's life.

Chapter 7:

Comprehensive Care and Support for Daughters

Picture this: You're standing in the aisle of your local drugstore, your daughter by your side, and you're both staring at an overwhelming array of feminine hygiene products. You can sense the awkwardness hanging in the air like a thick fog. Maybe you're thinking back to simpler times when playing tea party was the biggest challenge of the day. Yet here you are, tasked with helping your daughter make choices about menstrual health products and, later, navigating even more complex conversations about dating and safe sex. It's moments like these that can make any dad wish for a magic handbook on parenting.

But you know what? You're already holding that handbook, metaphorically speaking. In this final chapter, we'll explore how you can support your daughter through these significant and often challenging parts of growing up. You're not just her dad; you're her guide, her confidante, and her biggest advocate as she transitions from girlhood into womanhood.

Fostering open communication about self-care, relationships, and independence doesn't have to feel daunting. It's about normalizing these conversations at home so your daughter feels equipped to handle whatever life throws her way. This chapter will provide you with practical advice to ensure that your daughter grows into a well-rounded and empowered individual. From understanding the basics of self-care to navigating the complexities of emotional connections and asserting personal choices, we'll cover it all.

Let's start by setting the stage for a lifetime of honest and supportive dialogues, ensuring that these "awkward" topics become just another part of your regular father-daughter chats. Here's how you can create a safe space for both of you, filled with mindfulness, effective communication, and peaceful parenting.

The Foundation of Self-Care: Building Routines Together

When we think about self-care, we often imagine it as a personal journey, unique to each individual. But for fathers raising daughters, self-care is not just a personal responsibility—it's a shared one. From the toddler years to the tempests of teenage life and beyond, the self-care habits you help your daughter develop will lay the groundwork for her well-being throughout her life. In this section, we'll explore the basics of self-care across different life stages of your daughter's growth, emphasizing practices like personal hygiene that are vital for her health and self-esteem.

Early Childhood: Planting the Seeds of Self-Care

In the early years, your daughter is absorbing everything she sees and hears, and this is the perfect time to start introducing basic self-care routines. Think about simple habits like brushing teeth twice a day. For a young child, this can be turned into a fun and engaging activity rather than a chore. Sing songs, make up games, or even dance around the bathroom—whatever makes it enjoyable for both of you.

Handwashing is another essential habit to instill early on. With young children often exploring the world with their hands, teaching them to wash their hands properly is crucial. Explain the why as much as the how—talk about germs in a way that's understandable for a child, like "tiny bugs that we can't see but can make us feel sick." This helps them make sense of why we take the time to scrub our hands before meals, after playing outside, or when we come home from anywhere.

School-Age Children: Developing Independence

As your daughter grows and starts attending school, she'll begin to take more responsibility for her own self-care, but she'll still need your guidance. This is the stage to reinforce the routines already set and introduce new ones, such as skincare. Teaching her the basics of washing her face and using sunscreen can protect her skin and teach her the importance of routine care.

This is also the perfect time to start discussions about body changes and hygiene, which will be crucial during the coming pre-teen years. It's important to use actual anatomical names for body parts during these discussions. This practice promotes body positivity and empowers her with the correct vocabulary to express herself confidently about her health and body.

Make these conversations as natural and straightforward as discussing her day at school. This approach not only demystifies changes but also normalizes them, reinforcing that caring for her body is a normal part of life.

Adolescence: Navigating Changes Together

Adolescence brings about more significant and sometimes daunting changes for your daughter, especially concerning her body. This stage requires a delicate balance of privacy and parental involvement. Continue to foster open communication and be ready to support and update her self-care routines in response to her growing needs.

Menstrual health, for example, is a critical area. It's important to discuss not just the biological aspects but also how to manage it through personal hygiene. Encourage her to find what products she feels comfortable using, be it pads, tampons, or menstrual cups, and ensure she knows how to use them properly to maintain hygiene and health.

Start by explaining the different options available. Pads, for instance, are often the first go-to product for many young girls because they're straightforward to use. Tampons and menstrual cups can be introduced as she becomes more comfortable with her body. This can be a good time to stress the importance of changing these products regularly—about every 4–6 hours for tampons and every 12 hours for menstrual cups—to prevent any health issues such as infections or toxic shock syndrome.

Above all, normalize these discussions. The more openly and frequently you talk about menstrual health, the more you demystify and destigmatize it. Discuss the typical cycle, which can range from 21 to 35 days, and explain that bleeding usually lasts from 3 to 7 days. Help her track her cycle, either on a calendar or with an app. This helps her know when to expect her period and aids in recognizing any irregularities that might need a doctor's attention.

Provide her with a small kit that she can keep in her school bag—include a few pads or tampons, a fresh pair of underwear, and a small pack of wipes. This can help her feel prepared for any situation, reducing anxiety related to unexpected starts.

Moreover, it's crucial to talk about the emotional and physical changes that might accompany her period, such as cramps, mood swings, or fatigue. Understanding why these happen can reduce any fears or misconceptions she might have. For example, explaining that cramps are a result of the uterus contracting to help expel its lining can make them seem less daunting. You can also suggest ways to manage these symptoms, like using a warm heating pad for cramps or maintaining a healthy diet to help regulate her mood and energy levels.

Skincare might become more pertinent as issues like acne can appear. Support her in finding the right products that help manage her skin type. This can be a bonding activity, too, where you can learn together what works best for her skin, reinforcing that taking care of her appearance is about feeling good rather than just looking good.

Young Adulthood: Cultivating Lifelong Habits

As your daughter moves toward young adulthood, she'll be managing her self-care almost entirely on her own. However, your role as a father is still crucial. Continue to be a sounding board and a source of advice when she needs it. Encourage her to maintain the habits she has developed and to seek professional advice when necessary.

This stage is also about more than just physical self-care; it's about emotional and mental health. Encourage her to take time for herself, whether it's through hobbies, exercise, or simply relaxing. Discuss the importance of mental health openly, making sure she knows that it's okay to ask for help and to take care of her mind just as much as her body.

Through all these stages, remember that one of the best ways to teach your daughter about self-care is to model it yourself. Show her through your actions that taking care of oneself is a vital part of living a healthy, happy life. When you respect your own health, you set an example for her to follow, and this mutual respect for self-care becomes a cornerstone of your relationship.

By building these routines together, you're not just helping your daughter learn how to take care of her body and mind; you're strengthening your bond with her, showing her that you respect her growing independence, and providing her with the tools to thrive on her own. This shared journey of self-care is one of the most precious gifts you can give her, filled with lessons that will support her well-being for a lifetime.

Navigating the Waters of Dating and Relationships: A Guide for Fathers

Talking about dating, relationships, and safe sex with your daughter can seem daunting. You might wonder how to start such conversations and when. It's all about setting the stage for open, honest discussions that help her navigate these aspects of her life with confidence, respect, and safety. This section will guide you through framing these topics appropriately for different life stages, ensuring that your daughter feels empowered to make informed decisions about her relationships and health.

Early Conversations: Laying the Groundwork

Before your daughter even begins to show interest in dating, start laying the groundwork. Introduce the idea of respect within any relationship, be it with family, friends, or later romantic interests. Discuss what respect looks like: listening to each other, valuing opinions, and treating each other with kindness. These early conversations set a standard for how she should expect to be treated by others and how she should treat others in return.

When she starts to show interest in deeper friendships or early forms of dating, it's a great time to discuss what it means to enjoy someone's company. Emphasize that dating is essentially about getting to know someone better and enjoying time together. It's a journey of discovery where it's perfectly okay to say "no" at any stage. Teach her that any relationship should bring joy and respect, and if she ever feels uncomfortable, she has every right to step back or end it.

Teen Years: Deepening the Dialogue

As your daughter moves into her teen years, your conversations should evolve into more detailed discussions about dating and what healthy relationships look like. This includes talking about mutual interests, shared respect, and individual independence within a relationship. It's important to stress that a healthy relationship doesn't compromise one's own needs for the sake of the other's.

This is also the right time to discuss the physical aspects of relationships. It's crucial to be candid about pregnancy, sexually transmitted diseases (STDs), and safe sex practices. Educate her on the biological aspects and prevention methods. This might include a discussion on contraceptives, the importance of protection, and the right to access healthcare related to sexual and reproductive health.

Make sure to involve her in decisions regarding her health and emphasize her autonomy over her body. This includes the concept of ongoing consent, which is fundamental. Explain that consent is an active, ongoing process, and just because someone consents to one activity doesn't mean they consent to others. Consent can also be withdrawn at any time, and this should be respected without question.

Young Adulthood: Continuing Support

As your daughter grows into young adulthood, keep these conversations going. At this stage, discussions can become more nuanced and tailored to her experiences. She might face different challenges as she explores more serious relationships or even navigates the complexities of adult dating.

Continue to be a source of support and advice, but also respect her growing independence. She might not always want to share every detail with you, and that's okay. What's important is that she knows she can come to you when she needs advice or help.

Practical Tips for Fathers

- **Be approachable:** Always keep the door open for discussions. Let her know she can come to you with any questions or concerns without fear of judgment or punishment.

- **Educate yourself:** Be informed about the current realities of dating, including online dating and social media influences. This will help you stay relevant and empathetic to her experiences.

- **Provide resources:** Sometimes, direct conversations can be hard. Provide her with resources—books, articles, or websites—that can answer her questions or provide guidance in a less direct way.

- **Share your values:** While it's important to respect her independence, sharing your values regarding relationships and sex can guide her as she makes her own decisions.

- **Model respectful behavior:** Demonstrate through your actions how to respect women and maintain healthy relationships in your own life. This is one of the most powerful lessons you can give her.

Learning about dating and relationships is a crucial part of your daughter's journey to adulthood. By having open, honest, and respectful conversations, you empower her to make informed decisions that respect her body and emotions. Remember, the goal isn't to control or dictate her choices but to support her in making safe and respectful ones. Your role as a guide and confidante in these matters is invaluable, and it will help shape the way she views and handles relationships throughout her life.

Championing Choices: Creating a Supportive Environment for Your Daughter's Autonomy

Supporting your daughter in making her own decisions, especially regarding personal aspects like dating, being single, or her sexual orientation, is a profound way to empower her. Remember our discussion in Chapter 5 about empowering autonomy and confronting gender stereotypes? We focused on recognizing and dismantling these stereotypes to encourage your daughter to explore her full potential. Now, let's extend that empowerment into the realms of personal relationships and identity.

Embracing Her Choices in Relationships and Sexual Orientation

As a father, one of the most significant impacts you can have is supporting your daughter in the choices she makes about relationships. Whether she chooses to date, remain single, or explore anything in between, your support can help her feel secure in those decisions. It's essential to validate her feelings and choices, showing that her value does not depend on her relationship status.

When it comes to dating, ensure that your conversations don't just focus on the mechanics of "how to date" but also on the why, or possibly why not. Encourage her to reflect on what she genuinely wants from her relationships. Does she want to date right now? What does she value in a partner? Is she feeling pressured by friends or media to be in a relationship? These questions can help her make decisions that are truly right for her, not just conforming to societal expectations.

If she decides to remain single, champion that choice as well. Singlehood, especially for young women, can be a time of immense personal growth, self-discovery, and independence. Support her in pursuing her interests and passions without the distraction or compromise that sometimes comes with a relationship.

Sexual orientation is another deeply personal aspect of your daughter's identity. If she confides in you about her orientation, the way you respond can significantly impact her self-esteem and mental health. It's crucial to listen with an open heart and without judgment. Your acceptance and unconditional love can make all the difference in her feeling safe and valued in her own home.

Encouraging Career Exploration Beyond Gender Norms

Just as we discussed in Chapter 5, dismantling gender stereotypes extends to career choices as well. Whether your daughter shows interest in engineering, coding, art, or caregiving, every field should be open for her exploration without bias. Encourage her to pursue passions and interests that excite and challenge her, regardless of the traditional gender dominance in those fields.

For instance, if she shows an interest in a field traditionally dominated by men, such as aerospace engineering, support her curiosity and provide her with resources and role models in that sector. Conversely, if she wants to enter a field typically dominated by women, such as nursing or teaching, equally champion these choices. The key is to support her aspirations based on her interests and strengths, not societal expectations.

Creating an Empowering Home Environment

Your home environment plays a crucial role in how your daughter perceives her choices and opportunities.

Make your home a place where open conversations about careers, relationships, and identity are not just welcomed but encouraged. Show interest in her thoughts and feelings, and provide a nonjudgmental space where she can express her doubts and dreams.

Part of creating this environment is also reflecting on your own biases and working actively to dismantle them. Recognize that even well-meaning comments can sometimes reinforce stereotypes. Be conscious of how you discuss these topics, not just with her but with others in her presence. Your behavior models how she should expect others to treat her and sets the baseline for what she believes is possible for herself.

Empowering Your Daughter With Practical Skills

When you teach your daughter practical skills, you are preparing her to be self-sufficient and empowering her to tackle the world with confidence, independence, and creativity. From cooking to home repairs to managing her finances, these skills equip her to make informed decisions and take control of her own life. Let's discuss how you can guide her in mastering these essential skills.

Cooking: Cultivating Culinary Confidence

Starting with cooking, this skill is fundamental not just for survival but for healthy living. Begin with the basics: Teach her how to measure ingredients accurately, which is not only essential for cooking but also a great way to incorporate practical math skills. Next, move on to knife skills, teaching her how to chop, dice, and slice safely. It's important to supervise initially, but as she gets more comfortable, step back and let her take the lead.

Progress to teaching her how to handle various cooking methods such as boiling, sautéing, baking, and grilling. Each technique can be introduced with simple recipes. For instance, boiling pasta, sautéing vegetables, or baking a simple cake. As she masters each method, encourage her to experiment with recipes that interest her.

Include her in meal planning and shopping, which teaches her to think ahead and make decisions about nutrition and budget. This holistic approach not only builds her cooking skills but also her planning and organizational skills, boosting her confidence and independence in the kitchen.

Home Repairs: Promoting Self-Sufficiency

When it comes to home repairs, start by familiarizing her with basic tools—what each tool is called, what it's used for, and how to handle it safely. Begin with simple tasks like tightening screws, measuring and cutting straight lines, or changing batteries in household devices. These tasks may seem small, but they are the building blocks of more complex skills.

Gradually introduce more challenging projects, such as fixing a leaky faucet, painting a room, or assembling furniture. These tasks teach problem-solving and technical skills that will serve her throughout life. They also demystify the often male-dominated world of home repairs, showing her that she can manage her living environment without depending on others.

Encourage her to ask questions and seek out resources like online tutorials or workshops. This not only helps her gain more knowledge but also teaches her the importance of continuous learning and resourcefulness.

Financial Independence: Building Financial Savvy

Financial literacy is possibly one of the most critical skills you can teach your daughter. Start with the basics of budgeting. Show her how to track her income and expenses and how to plan for savings. This can begin with something as simple as managing an allowance or a savings account.

As she grows older, introduce more complex concepts like taxes, insurance, and credit. Use real-life scenarios to explain these concepts, such as discussing the family budget or showing her how to read a bank statement. This transparency educates her and involves her in family financial planning, showing her its relevance and importance.

Investing is another crucial area. Teach her about different types of investments—stocks, bonds, mutual funds, ETFs—and how each works. If possible, simulate investment scenarios or use online investment games to make the learning process interactive and fun.

Encourage her to set financial goals, whether saving for a new gadget, college, or eventually her own home. Discuss different strategies to achieve these goals, enhancing her understanding of financial planning and delayed gratification.

You're preparing your daughter to be independent and empowering her to take responsibility for her life by teaching her practical skills in cooking, home repairs, and financial management. These skills foster creativity, resilience, and adaptability, traits that will help her navigate the complexities of adulthood.

Remember, the goal is to make these learning processes enjoyable and informative, turning them into opportunities for bonding and growth. Think back to the visualization exercises we explored earlier—not just as a simple activity, but as a practice to foster your daughter's development into the capable and confident woman she will become.

Each skill you teach her adds another layer to her independence, shaping her into a capable and confident individual ready to face the world head-on. Celebrate each milestone in her learning journey, and watch as she transforms into a self-reliant, savvy, and skilled young woman.

Practical Exercises and Reflections

Supporting your daughter's growth involves more than just conversations; it involves practice and reflection that reinforce the concepts you discuss together. Below, you'll find practical exercises and reflection questions designed to help both of you engage deeply with topics like hygiene, dating, consent, and health. These activities can be incredibly beneficial in building her confidence and clarity in navigating these areas.

Decision-Making Trees

These are visual tools that help map out possible choices and their consequences, allowing for a structured approach to making informed decisions. Here's how you can use them in different contexts:

- **Hygiene decisions exercise:** Create a decision-making tree for choosing personal hygiene products. Start with the type of product (soap, shampoo, deodorant), then move to specifics like scents, ingredients, and brands. Discuss the implications of each choice, such as environmental impact, skin sensitivity, and cost.

- **Dating decisions exercise:** Work together to draw out a decision-making tree for responding to various social scenarios, such as being asked to a dance or handling a breakup. Include branches for saying yes, saying no, and asking for time to think, with outcomes and potential emotional responses for each.

- **Health decisions exercise:** Develop a decision-making tree for handling a day when she's feeling unwell and has commitments like school and extracurricular activities. Include pathways for different symptoms (e.g., headache, stomachache) and decisions like resting, seeing a doctor, informing teachers, or continuing with activities and scheduling time for rest afterward.

Problem-Solving Workshops

- **Scenario-based problem-solving exercise:** Set up scenarios that require problem-solving skills related to hygiene, health, and relationships. For instance, what she might do if she forgets her sports kit on a game day or how to handle a friend who is spreading rumors. Discuss various outcomes based on different approaches to solving these problems.

- **Role-switching debates exercise:** Debate a topic where you both take opposite views, then switch roles. Topics could be related to autonomy in teen years, like curfews or privacy.

This helps develop empathy and understanding of different perspectives, enhancing her communication and critical thinking skills.

Critical Thinking Challenges

- **What would you do?** Play a game where you describe a scenario, and she has to think of the best course of action. Scenarios might include seeing someone being bullied, finding a lost wallet, or dealing with peer pressure about risky behaviors. Discuss the reasons behind her decisions to deepen her understanding of her values and ethics.

- **Exploring consequences exercise:** Discuss hypothetical situations and explore all possible consequences of a single decision. For example, if she chooses to spend her entire allowance in one go, what might be the long-term effects? This exercise helps her understand the importance of foresight and planning in financial literacy and life choices.

Emotional Intelligence Role-Plays

- **Handling emotional situations:** Create role-play scenarios that involve managing emotions, such as anger or disappointment. For example, how to react when she doesn't make a team she tried out for, or how to handle feelings of jealousy. Role-playing these situations can help her develop emotional intelligence and resilience.

- **Empathy-building exercises:** Have discussions where you each share how you would feel in certain emotional situations, like if a friend moved away or if she faced a tough day at school. This helps build empathy and communication skills, key components of strong relationships.

These exercises are designed to be both fun and educational, providing safe spaces for your daughter to learn and grow. You'll help her develop a tool kit of skills that will enable her to navigate the complexities of life with confidence and wisdom by regularly engaging in these activities. Plus, these shared activities can strengthen your bond, making your time together both valuable and enjoyable.

Wrapping Up

You've made it through the journey of learning how to foster a nurturing, supportive, and empowering environment for your daughter. By now, you've grasped the essence of being not just a parent but a guide through the myriad complexities of growing up. From the aisles of supermarkets looking at hygiene products to having those first awkward talks about dating and health, each step has brought you closer and made your relationship stronger.

Remember, the foundation of all these lessons is the open and honest dialogue you maintain with her. It's these conversations that turn potential awkward moments into opportunities for growth and connection. Keep these dialogues going, be patient, and listen actively. Your role is crucial, and your impact is profound.

Conclusion

Congratulations on reaching this significant milestone in enhancing your relationship with your daughter. Through the insights and exercises in this book, you've embarked on an enduring process of growth and connection. You now stand with a new understanding of mindful parenting and communication, poised to impact your daughter's life positively.

Reflect on the transformation you've experienced since the beginning. Starting with understanding the nervous systems and stress responses in Chapter 1, you've built a foundation for a calm and composed approach to parenting. By engaging with the exercises, you have begun to model the emotional regulation skills that will serve your daughter throughout her life.

As you applied the practices from Chapter 2, you learned the value of presence and mindfulness in everyday interactions, providing a stable and supportive environment for your daughter. Chapter 3 invited you to explore your parenting influences, helping you to craft a more nurturing approach that reflects your deepest values.

Your journey through Chapter 4 revealed the power of mindful communication, fortifying your bond and ensuring that you remain connected even in today's digital age. In Chapter 5, you embraced strategies that foster your daughter's autonomy and resilience, preparing her to thrive in a gender-equal world.

Chapter 6 prepared you to support your daughter through any trauma with sensitivity and strength, ensuring she feels secure and valued. And in Chapter 7, you gained the tools to guide her through life's critical stages with care and wisdom.

Your role is pivotal. Every conversation, every shared moment, and every supportive gesture helps shape your daughter into a confident, resilient, and independent woman. The impact of your actions, big or small, cannot be overstated.

This book offered foundational tools and practices that will evolve as you and your daughter grow together. As you implement these strategies, view each as a step in an ongoing process of personal and relational growth. Challenges and setbacks are natural and can be faced with the knowledge and skills you've started to develop here.

Continue to adapt, learn, and grow. Your support and understanding create a space where she can thrive—no magic handbook required, just the heartfelt commitment to walking alongside her every step of the way.

If you found the insights and strategies in this book helpful, please consider leaving a review. Your feedback is invaluable. It not only helps improve the book but also supports other fathers in discovering this resource, empowering them to forge stronger bonds with their daughters.

References

Aas, M., Ueland, T., Inova, A., Melle, I., Andreassen, O. A., & Steen, N. E. (2020). Childhood trauma is nominally associated with elevated cortisol metabolism in severe mental disorder. *Frontiers in Psychiatry*, *11*. https://doi.org/10.3389/fpsyt.2020.00391

Active listening. (n.d.). People & Culture. https://hr.berkeley.edu/active-listening

Carolan, B. V., & Wasserman, S. J. (2015). Does parenting style matter? concerted cultivation, educational expectations, and the transmission of educational advantage. *Sociological Perspectives*, *58*(2), 168–186. https://doi.org/10.1177/0731121414562967

Cherry, K. (2023, June 29). *Emotions and types of emotional responses.* Verywell Mind. https://www.verywellmind.com/what-are-emotions-2795178

Crichton-Stuart, C. (2023, January 12). *What are the benefits of eating healthy?* Medical News Today. https://www.medicalnewstoday.com/articles/322268

Cross, D., Fani, N., Powers, A., & Bradley, B. (2017). Neurobiological development in the context of childhood trauma. *Clinical Psychology: Science and*

Practice, *24*(2), 111–124. https://doi.org/10.1111/cpsp.12198

Dewar, G. (2024, April 25). *The authoritative parenting style: An evidence-based guide.* Parenting Science. https://parentingscience.com/authoritative-parenting-style/

Franklin, B. A., Rusia, A., Haskin-Popp, C., & Tawney, A. (2021). Chronic stress, exercise and cardiovascular disease: Placing the benefits and risks of physical activity into perspective. *International Journal of Environmental Research and Public Health*, *18*(18), 9922. https://doi.org/10.3390/ijerph18189922

Gainer, D., Alam, S., Alam, H., & Redding, H. (2020). A flash of hope: Eye movement desensitization and reprocessing (Emdr) Therapy. *Innovations in Clinical Neuroscience*, *17*(7-9), 12–20.

Hodgdon, H. B., Anderson, F. G., Southwell, E., Hrubec, W., & Schwartz, R. (2021). Internal Family Systems (IFS) therapy for posttraumatic stress disorder (PTSD) among survivors of multiple childhood trauma: A pilot effectiveness study. *Journal of Aggression, Maltreatment & Trauma*, *31*(1), 22–43. https://doi.org/10.1080/10926771.2021.2013375

Murray, E. A., & Fellows, L. K. (2021). Prefrontal cortex interactions with the amygdala in primates. *Neuropsychopharmacology*, *47*(1), 163–

179. https://doi.org/10.1038/s41386-021-01128-w

Murray, H., Grey, N., Warnock-Parkes, E., Kerr, A., Wild, J., Clark, D. M., & Ehlers, A. (2022). Ten misconceptions about trauma-focused CBT for PTSD. *The Cognitive Behaviour Therapist, 15*. https://doi.org/10.1017/s1754470x22000307

Pace-Schott, E. F., Amole, M. C., Aue, T., Balconi, M., Bylsma, L. M., Critchley, H., Demaree, H. A., Friedman, B. H., Gooding, A. E. K., Gosseries, O., Jovanovic, T., Kirby, L. A. J., Kozlowska, K., Laureys, S., Lowe, L., Magee, K., Marin, M.-F., Merner, A. R., Robinson, J. L., & Smith, R. C. (2019). Physiological feelings. *Neuroscience & Biobehavioral Reviews, 103*, 267–304. https://doi.org/10.1016/j.neubiorev.2019.05.002

Pardee, L. (2024, February 22). *What is your parenting style, and why does it matter?* Parents. https://www.parents.com/parenting/better-parenting/style/parenting-styles-explained/

Peverill, M., Rosen, M. L., Lurie, L. A., Sambrook, K. A., Sheridan, M. A., & McLaughlin, K. A. (2023). Childhood trauma and brain structure in children and adolescents. *Developmental Cognitive Neuroscience, 59*, 101180. https://doi.org/10.1016/j.dcn.2022.101180

Rasouli, A., Heydari, H., Alyasin, S. A., & Abdi, M. (2018). Relationship between father's emotional intelligence and marital satisfaction with adolescent self-esteem and mental health. *Global Journal of Guidance and Counseling in Schools: Current Perspectives*, *8*(3), 165–172. https://doi.org/10.18844/gjgc.v8i3.3934

Salamon, M. (2023, July 7). *What is somatic therapy?*. Harvard Health Publishing. https://www.health.harvard.edu/blog/what-is-somatic-therapy-202307072951

Sansone, A. (2024). The central role of Mindful Parenting in child's emotional regulation and human flourishing: A blueprint perspective. *Frontiers in Psychology*, *15*. https://doi.org/10.3389/fpsyg.2024.1420588

Santoniccolo, F., Trombetta, T., Paradiso, M. N., & Rollè, L. (2023). Gender and media representations: A review of the literature on gender stereotypes, objectification and sexualization. *International Journal of Environmental Research and Public Health*, *20*(10), 5770. https://doi.org/10.3390/ijerph20105770

Santos, A. F., Fernandes, C., Fernandes, M., Santos, A. J., & Veríssimo, M. (2022). Associations between emotion regulation, feeding practices, and preschoolers' food consumption. *Nutrients*, *14*(19), 4184. https://doi.org/10.3390/nu14194184

Schroeder, K., Noll, J. G., Henry, K. A., Suglia, S. F., & Sarwer, D. B. (2021). Trauma-informed neighborhoods: Making the built environment trauma-informed. *Preventive Medicine Reports*, *23*,

101501. https://doi.org/10.1016/j.pmedr.2021.101501

Sharry, J. (2024, January 24). *How parental stress can affect a child's mental health*. SilverCloud® by Amwell®. https://www.silvercloudhealth.com/uk/blog/how-parental-stress-can-affect-a-childs-mental-health-silvercloud-by-amwell

Szadvári, I., Ostatníková, D., & Babková Durdiaková, J. (2023). Sex differences matter: Males and females are equal but not the same. *Physiology & Behavior, 259*, 114038. https://doi.org/10.1016/j.physbeh.2022.114038

Turpyn, C. C., Chaplin, T. M., Fischer, S., Thompson, J. C., Fedota, J. R., Baer, R. A., & Martelli, A. M. (2019). Affective neural mechanisms of a parenting-focused mindfulness intervention. *Mindfulness, 12*(2), 392–404. https://doi.org/10.1007/s12671-019-01118-6

Vandekerckhove, M., & Wang, Y. (2018). Emotion, emotion regulation and sleep: An intimate relationship. *AIMS Neuroscience, 1*(1), 1–22. https://doi.org/10.3934/neuroscience.2018.1.1

Zhang, Y., Fu, R., Sun, L., Gong, Y., & Tang, D. (2019). How does exercise improve implicit emotion regulation ability: Preliminary evidence of mind-body exercise intervention combined with aerobic jogging and mindfulness-based yoga. *Frontiers in Psychology, 10*. https://doi.org/10.3389/fpsyg.2019.01888

Printed in Dunstable, United Kingdom

70895331R00107